MW01412675

REDUCING ANXIETY OF PERSONS PRACTICING PASTORAL CARE

A COMPREHENSIVE GUIDE TO INTERPATHIC TRAINING

Dr. Dorothy Smith-Hubbard

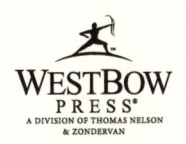

WESTBOW PRESS®
A DIVISION OF THOMAS NELSON
& ZONDERVAN

Copyright © 2017 Dr. Dorothy Smith-Hubbard.

All rights reserved. No part of this book may be used or reproduced by any means, graphic, electronic, or mechanical, including photocopying, recording, taping or by any information storage retrieval system without the written permission of the author except in the case of brief quotations embodied in critical articles and reviews.

Stamps, D. (1992). Full life study Bible. Grand Rapids, MI: Life Publishers International

Scripture taken from the King James Version of the Bible.

WestBow Press books may be ordered through booksellers or by contacting:

WestBow Press
A Division of Thomas Nelson & Zondervan
1663 Liberty Drive
Bloomington, IN 47403
www.westbowpress.com
1 (866) 928-1240

Because of the dynamic nature of the Internet, any web addresses or links contained in this book may have changed since publication and may no longer be valid. The views expressed in this work are solely those of the author and do not necessarily reflect the views of the publisher, and the publisher hereby disclaims any responsibility for them.

Any people depicted in stock imagery provided by Thinkstock are models, and such images are being used for illustrative purposes only. Certain stock imagery © Thinkstock.

ISBN: 978-1-9736-0443-3 (sc)
ISBN: 978-1-9736-0445-7 (hc)
ISBN: 978-1-9736-0444-0 (e)

Library of Congress Control Number: 2017915829

Print information available on the last page.

WestBow Press rev. date: 11/14/2017

CONTENTS

Dedication ix
Preface xi
Acknowledgements xiii

Chapter 1:   Introduction 1
Chapter 2:   Biblical-Theological-Historical Base 8
Chapter 3:   Theological Analysis of the Ministry of Presence.... 19
Chapter 4:   Theological Analysis of Hope 22
Chapter 5:   Theological Analysis of Mercy 26
Chapter 6:   Role of the Church Fathers in Pastoral Care 29
Chapter 7:   Theology of Modern Feminist & Womanist
             Perspectives 32
Chapter 8:   Theology of Pastoral Care across Cultures 36
Chapter 9:   What is Anxiety? 39
Chapter 10: Methodology 52
Chapter 11: Interpathic Training Assessment Survey
             Population Sample 57
Chapter 12: Interpretation & Response & Findings 67
Chapter 13: Theological Reflections 76

Appendix A. Flyer For Complimentary Course 83
Appendix B. Demographic Survey Assessment 84
Appendix C. Application For Research Project 85
Appendix D. Training, Providers, Target Group, Components.. 89
Appendix E. Desired Goals, Behavior Questions 90
Appendix F. IPT Syllabus Lesson Plan I & II 91
Appendix G. IPT Syllabus Lesson Plan I & II 93
Appendix H. IPT Syllabus Lesson Plan I & II 95
Appendix I. IPT Syllabus Lesson Plan I & II
             Sympathy, Empathy and Compassion 97

Appendix J. IPT Syllabus Lesson Plan I & II
　　　　　　　A Narrative Story 99
Appendix K. IPT Syllabus Lesson Plan I & II Trio-Logical 102
Appendix L. IPT Syllabus Lesson
　　　　　　　Interpathic Pastoral Care I & II 104
Appendix M. Attendance Sheet For Participants 106
Appendix N. Certificate Of Achievement 107
Appendix O. My Dad's "Exhortation" 108
References 111

DEDICATION

This book is dedicated to Branches Inc., its Board Members and Advisors, Team Facilitators, Ministry Partners and Volunteers who have made significant contributions to this ministry.

PREFACE

One of the revealing aspects that motivated the development of this research project, "Reducing Anxiety of Persons Practicing Pastoral Care through Interpathic Training," has been to experience the correlation between reducing one's personal anxiety and effectively practicing pastoral care to others. Since infancy my life has been riddled by an overwhelming shadow of anxiety. Health issues surrounding my birth, teen pregnancy, high school dropout, and divorce contributed to a feeling of unworthiness, which produced anxiety. As a result, years were spent seeking to attain validation and approval through others. The journey to uncover the inner anxiety issues relating to the development of an unhealthy personal identity was resolved through this research project. The pastoral care ministry began to flow more effectively when the anxiety from my personal identity was resolved. My journey of discovery can be seen throughout the following six chapters. This research project is aimed to provide clergy and laypersons a tool of training to use in reducing anxiety in practicing pastoral care. This research is a result of over thirty years of interpathic training, having discussions with experts in pastoral care, including detailed feedback and discussions with clergy, laypersons, and professionals.

ACKNOWLEDGEMENTS

I offer praises to Father God, who has created me in his image, Jesus Christ his son, who has given me eternal life, and the Holy Spirit, who has given wisdom by directing gifted people to cross my path. In memory of my loving parents; the Rev. Winfred C. Smith (Dad) and Marjorie Knowles Smith (Mom) who has provided the fire that flames my inspiration. To Roland C. Hubbard, Sr., my husband for his unconditional loving support. To my daughters; Christa, Dawn, Myra, and Charity, whom I birthed and who are treasured gifts. To my father-in-law; Flemon C. Hubbard, for his unending prayers. Gwen, Wenfer, Jessie, Michelle (sisters). Seth Wayne, Craig, Tony (brothers).

To Thaddeus Eastland, Senior Pastor and Dr. Desiree' Eastland (First Lady) Hope Church Pearland, TX.

To Jack Judy's continual support. To Pastors David & Carletta Douglas, Pastor Deborah Giles, Pastor Jacques Wigginton, Janice Brown, Dr. Ruth Ollison, Lee Family (Frankie, Katie, Nikki), Lucian-Lachelle Taylor, Mythe Foster, Audrey McMorris, Dee Bohn, Kyra Storms, Deborah Thomas, Kathy Bradley, Paulette Johnson, and countless family and friends who have prayed and offered support. Special appreciation to Dean Thomson K. Matthew, Dr. John Thompson, the committee members; Dr. Edward Decker, Dr. Bill Buker, Dr. Kenneth Mayton, and Celine Butler, for their leadership and counsel. A special thanks to Judy Seitz and Paul Huber Asbury Theological Seminary Doctor of Ministry Program, Wilmore, KY, and the Oral Robert's University Business Center.

CHAPTER 1

INTRODUCTION

There is awareness in personal pastoral care that every individual at some point will struggle with a crisis. Pastoral care may encompass listening to the concerns expressed from aging parents, discussing health challenges with a recently hospitalized friend, or offering a prayer of encouragement to someone in distress. Deciding how to best support someone through the afore mentioned issues can create anxiety and may cause a reluctance to practice personal pastoral care.

It's important that one's fear and anxiety not deter him or her from entering the field of ministry. Training can be administered that will help in overcoming pastoral care pitfalls. Clergy can become vital in helping laity seek meaning and come to an understanding. Janet O. Hagberg and Robert A. Guelich's *The Critical Journey* reviews stages in one's own personal experiences that brings a person to a fulfilled life of faith in Christ. Hagberg states, "In broader circles, spirituality has come to mean an urge or power within us that drives us toward meaning for our lives" (Hagberg & Guelich, 2005, p. 2). A myth and common underlying assumption among clergy seems to be the misconception that any untrained Christian layperson can be effective in administering personal pastoral care to another. Culbreth, Brown, and Milne's theories provide credibility regarding the need for a personal pastoral care training program (Culbreth, Brown, & Milne, 2010). The preconceived myths from clergy and laypersons will be exposed through the implementation of this applied research method in this project.

There is an urgent need to obtain Interpathic Personal Pastoral Care (IPPC) training that will address the question, "How can anxiety be overcome when practicing personal pastoral care with others?" The problem is that many Christian laity have a desire to practice pastoral care, but are overwhelmed with anxiety and experience a reluctance to successfully move beyond a feeling of sympathy. There are various aspects of responsive expressions that laypersons may experience during a time of crisis. When someone experiences a crisis, the initial instinct is sympathy which is demonstrated by showing kindness to another. The next responsive expression relates to empathy, which begins by having an understanding, being considerate, and offering a general prayer that will bring comfort. The final and most significant responsive expression is called interpathic. According to Augsburger,

Interpathy enables one to enter a second culture cognitively and affectively, to perceive and conceptualize the internal coherence that links the element of the culture into a dynamic interrelatedness, and to respect that culture (with its strengths and weaknesses) as equally as valid as one's own. This interpathic respect, understanding, and appreciation makes possible the transcendence, for a moment in a care, of cultural limitations. (Augsburger, 1986, p.14) While sympathy is a spontaneous reaction to another's feelings and may prompt one to intentionally respond to another with understanding, it allows one to understand that an individual is hurting. Interpathic pastoral care causes one to go beyond one's anxiety and possible reluctance, to journeying with another until an encounter with the light of Jesus Christ's love will shine through, bringing transformation to another.

The purpose of the book is to help laypersons develop interpathic skills that will reduce their anxiety and reluctance to practice personal pastoral care in their local church and communities. The applied research project will investigate these two questions:

1. Can persons practicing pastoral care integrate interpathic training to facilitate interpathic pastoral care into one's daily routine?
2. Can a teaching series relating to Christian formation, critical journey (hitting the walls), abiding in the vine, trio-logical process, and application of narrative story reduce anxiety?

The rationale behind these questions is finding the proper perspective of what IPPC can offer to local churches and para-organizations. Overcoming the effects of anxiety in laity and reducing the cause of one's limitation to and reluctance to practice personal pastoral care would be a tremendous support to local pastors.

Hope Church Pearland, Texas was the setting for the research. It was conducted in the suburbs, approximately 20 miles on the outskirts of metropolitan Houston. It is a United Methodist Church comprised of 96% African American, 3% Asian and Caucasian, and 1% Hispanic. Weekly attendance in Sunday worship service is between 300 and 500. The senior pastor is a professional pastoral care counselor who conducts an interactive counseling model Bible study every Wednesday evening.

Theologically the church is non-traditional. The mission at HOPE is "saving souls, healing hurts and sharing hope" in the community. Hope Church Pearland's Sunday morning worship service is a blend of contemporary gospel Christian music. There are two pastoral care groups authorized to support and tend to the congregation's needs, Compassion Covenant Care (CCC) and Stephen's Ministry. These groups were developed because the congregational needs had grown beyond the Pastor and First Lady's capacity to handle the requests. The Pastor desires to develop a more personal pastoral care ministry approach that will expand to small groups (Matt 25:40).

The Pastor is focused on building men to become godly husbands and strong fathers who will also produce strong communities. The First Lady oversees the women's ministry and focuses on building up women and helping them discover a purpose and walk in their God-given destiny. This is accomplished through a weekly infusion conference prayer line and weekly biblical training program.

Branches Inc., a 501(c) (3) founded in 1992, by Dorothy Smith-Hubbard, is based upon a Christ-centered approach to train and equip lay leaders to serve their church and communities. Using a Christ-centered approach, its slogan reads, "Since driving is done best behind the wheel, leaders are raised up to serve their churches and communities through mentors." Branches Inc. provides pastoral care and leadership development programs such as seminar training, mission trips, and evangelistic outreach programs. The scripture that uses the metaphor portraying Christ as a vine and depicting the disciples as his body extending personal pastoral care to others is its foundational scripture (John 5:15).

The IPPC training program, which is part of Branches Inc., will help identify the specific cause of an individual's anxiety that may cause the person to become reluctant to administer pastoral care to others. When a person is properly trained in personal pastoral care, it also gives those residing in those communities a witness who acknowledges the presence of the unconditional love found in Christ. This IPPC training program will motivate believers to overcome their anxiety and reluctance to practice personal pastoral care with others. The training will facilitate a positive attitude in laypersons toward witnessing the love of Christ in various pastoral settings. It will multiply the number of caregivers by equipping and mobilizing laypersons to provide high-quality Christian care. It will strengthen the pastors of local churches and enable them to focus on other needs of the church. The IPPC training will be a powerful tool that will also support the mission and vision of any local church. It activates the love of Christ in the church family and community.

Professor Stephen Seamands, a colleague affiliated with the Asbury Theological Seminary, stated, "Taking risks as I seek to participate in God's mission never seems to get easier. Even God has proven himself faithful in the past and has blessed my steps of risky obedience, I am always scared" (Seaman's, 1989, p. 177). In ministering to others and extending oneself to help humanity involves taking sacrificial risks. The IPPC research will reveal how to reduce anxiety and enable more people to volunteer in the local church. Sky McCracken, a United Methodist Conference clergy leader, states, "There are a lot more laity than clergy who can extend personal pastoral care to another if properly trained" (McCracken, 2013). The result of this IPPC project will mobilize and equip laypersons with personal pastoral care skills that will cover more congregational pastoral needs. Laity who have obtained this interpathic personal pastoral training will implement the grace and compassion of God without anxiety to those who may be broken and spiritually wounded in the congregation. Henri Nouwen stated, "Ultimately, it is Christ in us from whom healing comes. Only Christ can break through our human alienation and restore the broken connections with each other and God" (Nouwen, 1977, p. 34). Lay leaders will be taught how to ask meaningful questions, exegeting persons, situations, and context when ministering to the wounded during a crisis. Participants will be equipped to intervene during a time of crisis and to use their skills to administer interpathically personal pastoral care to bereaved families, the sick, and shut-ins. Understanding the core essentials of the differences between sympathy, empathy, and interpathic is crucial to obeying the great commission mandated to the church through Jesus (Matt 28:19-20).

Edwin Friedman explains how difficult integrated perspectives of our personal and professional life can turn crises into opportunities and can move us into a direction of less stress and demanding times. Such times could include a critical illness or other traumas in life when we may experience high stress, which reduces our ability to cope. At these times, the help of others may be very valuable (Friedman, 1986, p. 1).

Pastoral care, in a general sense, refers to ministry and services usually performed by a pastor in a local church, hospital, home, and/or hospice care facilities. The Latin meaning of the word pastor is "shepherd." A shepherd is a caregiver to God's flock. Philip Keller states, "Now the beautiful relationships given to us repeatedly in Scripture between God and man are those of a father to his children and a shepherd to his sheep" (Keller, 1970, p. 16).

Interpathic pastoral care is the practice of interpathy. "Interpathy enables one to enter a second culture cognitively and affectively, to perceive and conceptualize the internal coherence that links the element of the culture into a dynamic interrelatedness, and to respect that culture (with its strengths and weaknesses) as equally as valid as one's own. This interpathic respect, understanding and appreciation makes possible the transcendence, for a moment in a particular care, of cultural limitations" (Augsburger, 1986, p.14).

Webster's New Collegiate Dictionary uses words and phrases such as "painful," "apprehensive," "uneasiness of mind," and "an abnormal overwhelming sense of apprehension" to describe anxiety (Merriam-Webster, 1974, p. 51). Anxiety that seems to be an overestimation of danger can cause an individual to express a reluctance to practice pastoral care. Allan Cole Jr. suggests that knowing more about anxiety helps in becoming skillful in working with others (Cole Jr., 2008).

The data will assist in facilitating an IPPC training technique that will impact laypersons to continue practicing pastoral care with respect to ongoing clergy support.

The IPPC training is limited to Hope Church Pearland. The church has the Compassionate Covenant Care group, to equip the church to reach out in compassion to families in bereavement, sickness in hospital settings, nursing homes, private homes, retirement communities, and hospice care during a time of crisis. The pastoral staff is limited in its ability to offer adequate pastoral care to the membership. It is necessary for laity to train to assist the pastor in reaching the needs of the church's growing congregation. This has provided an opportunity to specifically train clergy and laity to volunteer and serve the pastoral leadership at Hope Church Pearland.

It is assumed that there will be positive changes between the pre- and post-test results. These changes will reflect a reduction in the individual's level of anxiety showing that anxiety prior to testing was higher prior to IPPC training. The IPPC training program will highlight the importance of a supervisory servant leader through the facilitator's mentoring approach of Branches Inc. Laity members will identify their ministerial calling and learn how to implement their spiritual giftedness through Christian formation exercises, individual mentoring, and training sessions. The participants will orally share personal narratives and their Christian formation testimonies. Because of IPPC training, a measure of reassurance and confidence will reduce their anxiety in mentoring pastoral care.

This project is designed to help laity develop interpathic pastoral care through being trained in IPPC. The research will result in a decrease in anxiety to perform pastoral care. For some, their embedded theological perspectives may influence the roadblocks of practicing pastoral care. The concept of carrying out pastoral care responsibilities may produce anxiety in the minds of laypersons who may have been taught it is a sacred trust only for pastors.

The pre-competence assessments and post-competence assessments will reveal an attendee's understanding and anxiety levels before and after the training is completed. It is my desire to encourage and fulfill the Great Commission of Jesus Christ (Matt 28:19-20) through this journey of pastoral care training. When clergy and laity experience a reduction of anxiety by obtaining IPPC training so they can reach beyond themselves and offer grace and mercy to others, the light of Jesus Christ's love brings transformation.

CHAPTER 2

BIBLICAL-THEOLOGICAL-HISTORICAL BASE

To become anxious or fearful is a normal response when attempting an unfamiliar task or meeting an unfamiliar person. The Bible specifically mentions two types of fear. The first is the reverential awe of the presence of the Lord, which is beneficial (Ps 111:10). Parents want their children to respect and honor them. How much more does the creator of the universe, who is worthy of obtaining all the praise? There is a second, detrimental type of fear that is mentioned in Scripture as a tormenting type of fear (2 Tim 1:7). Dealing with unanticipated events such as a sudden death or illness, or budget cuts that may have led to termination of employment can also cause anxiety. The nature of God is perfect love, peace, and fullness of joy (1 John 4:18).

Unfortunately, unplanned circumstances can cause believers to question and doubt the validity of the word of God. Believers are admonished to fear not, in other words, not to become anxious about anything or anyone (Isa 41:10). Adam became fearful of God by disobeying the commands of God. This depicts the nature of fallen humanity (Gen 3:10). Adam's fear and anxiety was a result of guilt and sin which led to separation from God. There is a healthy fear that can bring comfort during anxiety. This fear is available to every individual, unconditionally. And who can bring joy during any sorrowful circumstance? God does not promise humanity to be exempt from anxiety or fear but promises to provide strength through all the storms of life. In light of the project's stated problem, reducing anxiety of persons practicing pastoral care through interpathic training, the following Old and New Testament biblical accounts reflect the possibility of persons experiencing potential anxiety. These case studies serve to demonstrate how dealing with a crisis has a potential of causing anxiety and limiting one's effectiveness in practicing pastoral care. The examples that are cited begin with the study of Jethro, an elderly father-in-law assisting his son-in-law (Exo. 8:1-24), the New Testament case study of the leadership of Jesus helping the disciples on the road to Emmaus (Luke 24:1-16), and the necessity and importance of abiding in relationship with Christ aids in reducing anxiety (John 15:1-5). Finally, the story of Ruth, a Moabite who joins Naomi, her Israelite mother-in-law, during a time of significant loss, reducing anxiety through a "interpatch" act of offering a prayer of concern and showing kindness to another during a time of crisis (Ruth 1:16-18, 20-21). Research has been conducted by David Augsburg, a professor of pastoral counseling at Fuller Theological Seminary relating to interpathic. He cited from his book, *Pastoral Counseling Across Cultures*: The intercultural counselor develops a special skill that is called interpathic. It enables one to enter a second culture, cognitively and affectively, to perceive and conceptualize the internal coherence that links the elements of the culture into a dynamic interrelatedness, and to respect that culture with its strength and weakness as equally valued as one's own. The interpathic respect of understanding and appreciation makes possible the transcendence, for a moment in a case of cultural limitations. (Augsburger, 1986, p. 27) This chapter will seek to provide Biblical accounts representing individuals who were able to partner with another to overcome and move beyond their anxiety to effectively implement interpathic pastoral care. Some questions this chapter will seek to address include:

- What does the Bible say in the Old and New Testament about pastoral care?
- What are the theological inferences of the ministry of presence, hope, and mercy as it relates to pastoral care?
- Historically, how did our church fathers handle the role of pastoral care?
- How does the Feminist & Womanist movement shape our pastoral perspective in this post-modern era?
- What is the gospel message cross-culturally in pastoral care?

Addressing these concerns will relate to how church leaders should proceed in forging a biblical, theological, and spiritual bridge whose priority is to reduce anxiety in pastoral care and to empower laity in the local church.

The book of Exodus represents the people of God's departure from an old lifestyle to a new way of finding freedom and adventure. It is a wonderfully practical study of God's Word written by Moses. It contains foundational truths about deliverance, redemption, the law, and the Tabernacle as God reveals insights for leaders through Moses. The study also contains the sacrifice made in Israelite families leaving to protect themselves from the wrath of Pharaoh while the Egyptians experienced the events of God's judgment. God commanded Moses to become his ambassador to deliver the Hebrews from Egyptian bondage and implement law and order after he obtained the Ten Commandments on Mt. Sinai (Exo. 31:18-20).

Moses' role of pastoral care is challenged by Jethro, his father-in-law. Jethro observed Moses and stated, "What is this you are doing for the people? Why do you alone sit as judge, while all these people stand around you from morning until evening?" (Exo. 18:14) Moses was worn. This may be interpreted as Moses being anxious and overwhelmed in administering leadership to Hebrew families (Exo. 18:17).

His father-in-law further stated, "If your method of judging the people continues, you will surely wear out" (Exo. 18:18). The meaning of "wear out," is to become old, consumed, decaying, to waste away (Strong's, 1989). If one is wearing out, it is easy to become anxious, apprehensive, and lose focus or comprehension. Jethro comes alongside and reaches beyond his normal scope of responsibilities to offer an effective alternative to Moses. He suggested:

> Select capable men from all the people—men who fear God, trustworthy men who hate dishonest gain—and appoint them as officials over thousands, hundreds, fifties and tens. Have them serve as judges for the people at all times, but have them bring every difficult case to you; the simple cases they can decide themselves. That will make your load lighter, because they will share it with you. If you do this and God so commands, you will be able to stand the strain, and all these people will go home satisfied. (Exo. 18: 21-23) Jethro's sound biblical advice demonstrates the process of interpathic pastoral care. Jethro goes beyond his comfort zone by transcending into Moses' environment to provide an objective technique that will reduce his anxiety and regain his strength (Exo. 18:23). Because Jethro had developed an Interpathic understanding, he helps Moses find a better method of working with the people of Israel that allows him to judge the people successfully (Exo. 18:19-25). The Book of Ruth provides an Old Testament view of a blended family dynamic of a daughter-in-law and mother-in-law demonstrating interpathic pastoral care because of a crisis. The book of Ruth has been known for its literary quality; it is short and consists of only four chapters. It is a beautifully composed narrative that depicts interpathic pastoral care. Scripture reveals how Ruth unites with Naomi through a season of

crisis. The Old Testament book of Ruth portrays theological elements from the loss of identity, perseverance, famine, survival, and provision that may have caused anxiety (Ruth 1:1-22). One of the greatest gifts that Ruth's relationship brought to Naomi was the ministry of presence (Ruth 1:17). Interpathic pastoral care involves commitment beyond saying a few kind words. Ruth's devotion to Naomi through her act of leaving her culture, country, and family to unite with Naomi's culture in Bethlehem reveals loyalty. This is an indispensable virtue in interpathic pastoral care.

The story of Ruth and Boaz intersects with Moses and Jethro's narrative in the following manner. Ruth and Jethro set aside their individual agendas to provide a redeeming act that impacted generations to come. As a result, both narratives focus on redemption, salvation, and deliverance of the people of God. The narrative begins with the Emmaus Village, which is 60 furlongs (stadia) from Jerusalem. The narrative occurs once in the Bible. The Biblical account in Luke has a four-part breakdown in structure of the text—the meeting (Luke 24:13-16), the disciples and Christ's conversation about recent events (24:17-27), the meal shared with the disciples that also reveals that Christ has been with the disciples all along during their walk (24:28-32), and the return and report of the event (24:33-35). Luke the physician and disciple of Christ pens a reliable and precise record of history (Luke 5:31, Col 4:14).

The majority of this New Testament synoptic account was written by Luke. Material that Luke writes is with such irony and skill as he provides details and drama concerning the following events. Two disciples are travelling to Emmaus village, about seven miles from Jerusalem. Many times, the names of the disciples of Jesus are shrouded. Nevertheless, Cleophas' name was given in Luke (v. 13). The first epistle to the Corinthians declares that Jesus, who has resurrected, appears before James (1 Cor 15:7). It was most troubling to them that the tomb of Jesus was empty. The tomb was without his body. This truly heightened their fear and brought a sense of anxiousness and hopelessness for the future (Luke 24:5). Myths throughout the region suggest that the disciples had stolen the body, or that the Pharisees—religious leaders of the day—took his body.

Speculation believed that Christ never died in the first place, bringing more trauma to the travelers. Christ draws near to the disciples (Luke 24:15) and joins them by walking alongside the disciples. Interpathic pastoral care is demonstrated by Jesus when he "drew near" to the disciples. The Greek word *eggizo* (#1448) translates to mean; "be at hand, come near and come nigh" (Strong's, 1881, p. 25). Author John Bevere urges the body of Christ, disciples should not settle for a dry, shallow relationship with Christ, but accept the incredible invitation from the creator of the universe to come close and become intimate with him (Bevere 2004). Christ invited the disciples to come close to him when he joined them on their journey. The term "draw near" is repeated (Luke 24:27-28) as Christ remunerates the account of Moses and what the prophets revealed about his death, burial, and resurrection (Luke 24:27-28). At this point, neither of the disciples recognized Christ until after their meal and communion with him. Then their eyes became open.

The interpathic pastoral care provider will be able to walk with another because he or she is abiding in the presence of Christ, the vine which relates to the ministry of presence. Christ is the source and strength of our lives as we abide in him. The realization that Jesus Christ was alive empowered the disciples to overcome their anxiety, regain restored faith and prepared them to become witnesses to the other disciples (Luke 24:29-35).

The metaphor of Christ abiding in the vine illustrated in the Gospel of John is a vital biblical account of how one can overcome anxiety and effectively minister pastoral care (John 15:1-5). The Gospel of John, the fourth gospel book, depicts the ministry of Jesus

Christ in the region of Judea and Jerusalem. Jesus trained his disciples to undergo harsh treatment and prepared them to face various trials and persecutions because of their stand against apostasy; however, the message that Jesus taught and modeled remained true. John reveals the personhood of Jesus, forth telling about his birth, death, burial, and resurrection. The Apostle John provides evidence that Jesus Christ indeed was Israel's Messiah and God's incarnated (not adopted) son (John 2:1-11; 4:46-54; 5:2-18; 6:1-15; 6:16-21; 9:1-41; 11:1-46).

Most scholars believe the Gospel of John reflects the concerns of second generation Christians coming from a time when the disciples were expecting Jesus, the Messiah, to liberate and overthrow the Roman government. The Romans had a superior view, and the hypocrisy of the Scribes and Pharisees hated Jesus and his followers. The disciples of Jesus were expecting him to overthrow the Roman government and rule the world (Stamps, 1992). The following is an outline of the breakdown of the gospel of John as it relates to the ministry of Jesus. The Gospel of John, chapters 1–12, conveys the incarnation and public ministry of Jesus. The Jews' rejection of Jesus as their Messiah was prophesied by the old covenant and is reflected in chapters 13–21. The last discourse of Jesus in chapters 14–16 and the final prayer of Jesus for his present disciples and those to come are written in chapter 17. The New Testament covenant that is established by Jesus Christ through his death in chapters 18–19, and the resurrection of Jesus Christ in chapters 20–21, all convey the ministry of Christ on the earth (Stamps, 1992).

Apostle John, the son of Zebedee and one of the twelve disciples, is traditionally considered the author of the fourth gospel book. The Gospel of John was written in AD 80-95 to a Jewish audience. It is recommended for new converts or new babies preparing to become disciples and followers of Jesus Christ. The gospel of John is also written to prepare Christians for spiritual growth and development. Christ and his disciples experienced great persecution because of false teachings. John clearly conveys the purpose of this gospel message and pastoral training of Jesus Christ was to strengthen his disciples and followers so, that they might believe that Jesus Christ is the son of God (John 20:31).

The literary context and analysis with the words "I am" (Greek word *sozo*) translates as "to save" (Strong's, pp.70). Some scholars say, "I am," ["*ego eimi*" (John 8:58)], Jesus is identifying himself as Yahweh, the God of Israel. Some suggest that Jesus was before Abraham, "I am" (John 8:56-58). Jesus pre-existed because he is the one almighty God, Yahweh, and Elohiym, who also spoke to Moses. God was the "I am" (Exo. 20:1-2). Hebrew scholars translated the Old Testament between the third and first centuries BC. The word Yahweh was interpreted differently. God was claiming the title of "The Being" or "The One who is" rather than the "I am," or *ego-eimi* in Greek (McKee, 1992).

Disciples who produce fruit for Christ will be able to bear more fruit (John 15:8). The fruits of the Spirit spring from the fruit of love, joy, peace, long-suffering, kindness, and mercy, that are required to become disciples of Christ (Gal 5:22-23). The disciples also are to bear and gather more fruit, meaning to multiply their efforts by duplicating the teaching of Christ in more disciples (John 15:6). The parable of the fig tree contrasts the importance of bearing and gathering fruit (Luke 13:6-9). There is a divine promise that when we remain and abide in Christ, we can ask what we will and it shall be done (John 15:7). When we are obedient to bear, and gather fruit for Christ, our prayers will be fervent and answered (James 5:16, 18). Ultimately, our goal as disciples will be to glorify Christ in bearing fruit as a recognition of the greatness of God (John 15:8).

The genre of John is a figurative metaphorical language in the verse "I am the true vine and my Father is the husbandman." He addresses his disciples to continue the process of becoming a disciple of Jesus Christ (John 15:1). There is a spiritual oneness and unity, represented in the Godhead (Father, Son, and Holy Spirit) that is represented in the metaphor of "the vine and branches." God is the gardener, vine-dresser, and the disciple's eternal Father (John 15:1,

4, 5) and the branches—the followers of Jesus Christ—reflect the personhood of Christ when they bear fruit for God (John 15:2, 5, 6).

Jesus uses the literary devices of fruit of the vine in his last supper before his death (Mark 14:23-25; Matt 26:27-29) to produce the drink for the last supper. We must analyze words in light of how the first-century audience would understand them. The Greek word for "vine or grapevine," is *ampelos*. This is referenced in the Parable of the Fig Tree: "Can a fig tree bear olives or grapevine bear figs?" (James 3:12). These are allegories, depicting an abstract concept (Rev 14:18). "Trust in your sharp sickle and gather the cluster of the vine of the earth for her grapes are fully ripe" is used and modified by the word grapes. Another Greek term, *ampelon*, deriving from the same word, *ampelos*, means "vineyard" (Arndt, G.F.W., & Danker, 1979).

The New Testament text uses the term "vineyard that is filled with grapes" (Matt 21:33-41; Mark 12:1-11; Luke 20:9-16). Indeed, the terms "vine" and "vineyard," are usually associated with grapes and wine made from the grapes. It is also interesting to denote that the first miracle Jesus Christ performed during his ministry happened when he turned water into wine at a marriage feast in Cana of Galilee (John 2:1-11). In Palestine, the vines were celebrated for luxuriant growth and for the immense clusters of grapes which were produced. Jesus uses grapes for the wine, instituting the Lord's Supper, as he speaks of the contents of the cup as the fruit of the vine (Mark 14:25).

Theological interpretation of the Old Testament prophets focused on the imagery of the fruit of the vine to illustrate the judgment of God and economic disorder (Isa 32:10-15). Vineyards were essential to the Jewish economy and well-being. According to tradition, after the judgment of the flood, Noah planted a vineyard to reflect the seed time and harvest; a time to plant seed, which represents a season of fruitfulness (Gen 8:22). It was also a symbolic gesture of God to encourage the people to move forward, to be fruitful, multiply, and replenish the earth (Gen 9:1). The importance of the vine in the earliest time in Israel represented peace and prosperity. As long as the people of God stayed connected to the vine, they would bear more fruit (Mic 4:4; Zech 3:10; 2 Kgs 18:31; Isa 36:16; Ps128:1-6).

Sal Ciresi, a noted scholar, reveals in his theological exposition of how Apostle John's writings reach a level of literary beauty difficult to surpass. The "vine and branches" represent a parable in the Greek meaning, "parabole." Parables are earthly stories with a heavenly meaning; they convey biblical messages of truth. John speaks of Christ as "the true" vine. In other words, Christ was real and authentic, not counterfeit but genuine (Vine, 1901).

In the beginning the "Word" or *Logos* was with God, denoting the incarnation of Christ began in the beginning of creation (John 1:1; 14:4). The image of God and his sovereignty are conveyed throughout the text. John portrays God the father, Christ his son, and the Spirit of God as the Trinity from the very beginning. Apostle Paul likens the Gentile Christians to branches of a wild olive tree that had to be engrafted into the cultivated olive tree to become part of the promised covenant.

The term, "people of God" is in the Old Testament and New Testament to depict the covenant that God had with his people. Christ gives us a new covenant in the Gospel of John, to love one another. Union with Christ and consequences of obeying Christ produces fruit. Christ describes himself as "the true vine and his disciples as the branches. Christ is the only way and the truth and life. The synoptic gospels, especially the book of John, is an atlas emanating pastoral care. Yet, the idea of fruit-bearing is not exclusively mandated in the Gospel of John. In the beginning, when the earth was created, God told mankind to be fruitful and multiply (Gen 1:28). Pastoral care derives from discipleship. Jesus trained the disciples on how to bear fruit by observing Christ's relationship with God and his father.

Christ spent three years training twelve laypersons how to become disciples through his precepts and example. In this post-modern era, theology of ministry must include the mandate of the Great Commission (Mark 16:15). In a nutshell, reducing anxiety—which may cause a reluctance to practice pastoral care—comes as we encounter a relationship with Christ Jesus. Christ trained his disciples how to practice pastoral care through his servant leadership training while on earth. His disciples carried out his example in the book of Acts. When the Grecian women were being neglected, disciples were selected to perform pastoral care duties (Acts 6:1-17). The church must be seen by the world as a living organism that manifests the glory of God on the earth. Experiencing an encounter with Christ will ignite a passion that will birth a hunger to abide in Christ and reduce a reluctance of approaching a stranger. Our union in Christ supersedes the fear that would normally cause a reluctance of practicing pastoral care.

By implementing an effective pastoral care training program, persons will overcome anxiety and a reluctance to practice pastoral care. Abiding in Christ relieves and overcomes anxiety by empowering disciples to move beyond the anxiety and minister to others in the community and local church. Interpathic pastoral care begins with having the obedience of Moses, the commitment of Ruth and the willingness to operate in faith as the disciples were continuing to walk on the road to Emmaus and abiding in the vine to remain faithful to Christ.

CHAPTER 3

THEOLOGICAL ANALYSIS OF THE MINISTRY OF PRESENCE

> Christ is the originator of the ministry of presence. For though we rely on the church as on the presence of God, we do so just in that the church within herself directs us to a presence of God that is not identical with herself. In a formula, we have already used and will often return to, the church is the body of Christ for the world and for her members, in that she is constituted a community by the verbal and visible presence to her of that same body of Christ. The body of Christ is at once his sacramental presence within the church's assembly, to make that assembly a community and is the church-community herself for the world and her members. (Jensen, 1999)

The incarnation demonstrates the value that Christ has placed on every soul. God sent his son, Jesus, to reflect his presence through his birth, death, resurrection, and return as revealed in scripture (John 3:16-17). God created the heavens and earth, sent Christ to redeem humanity, and released the Holy Spirit to be present with his disciples until Christ returns. In 1933, Bonhoeffer, a theologian who embodied the passion to disciple students at Finkenwalde Seminary in Germany, delivered a message to a crowd in Berlin. He stated,

"Christ's proclamation promises his witness and presence which is a gift to humanity he was able to perform" (Bonhoeffer, 1985).

In other words, the ministry of presence is not just one type of ministry alongside others, it is the first and last word in any ministry that understands itself as an authentic response to a compassionate God. The word "compassion" originally comes from two Latin roots, *cum* ("with") and *pati* ("to suffer")—thus, "to suffer with." The idea is that one individual enters the hurt and suffering of another with true feelings and solidarity (Stone, 1996).

On the road to Emmaus, Christ—a stranger—introduces the ministry of presence to the disciples. Cleophas and friend share with the stranger a series of events that has triggered a sense of anxiousness in them. The ministry of presence is not always agreeing with what another state but to challenge that person through dialogue to bring truth to the surface. Christ first accepts the disciples, listens to their concerns, and later validates them with his acts of compassion (Luke 24:14-27).

The disciples were comforted by the ministry of presence with Christ; they begged him to remain with them (Luke 24:29). Jesus not only went to their homes, he communed with them until their eyes were open to the truth. The ministry of presence is to be there, to hurt, and to feel with them. It is much more than a general benevolence or pleasant disposition of compassion. As Salvadoran priest Jon Sobrino said, it is to "internalize" the suffering of others (Sobrino, 1993). God, through Christ, enters intimate community with us, and at the same time, struggles with us out of his compassion. His presence in our lives is the central framework for an authentic compassionate ministry in our world today. Our theology and how we practice or carry out the ministry of compassion should be consistent, explicit, and clear (Murray, 2007).

God is present always in us, but many times ministry goes beyond just one's simple observation. The ministry of presence should stretch one to become intimately involved with another.

Reducing Anxiety of Persons Practicing Pastoral Care

> In a time so filled with methods and techniques designed to change people, to influence their behavior, and to make them do new things and think new thoughts, we have lost the simple but difficult gift of being present to each other . . . simply being with someone is difficult because it asks of us that we share in the other's vulnerability, enter with him or her into the experience of weakness and powerlessness, become part of uncertainty, and give up control and self-determination. And still, whenever this happens, new strength and new hope being born. (Nouwen, 1982)

When Dad was diagnosed with terminal cancer he became anxious and unable to sleep because of dealing with his own mortality. The ministry of presence may require dealing with one's weakness, especially when administering interpathic pastoral care with family members. Dad was always a tower of strength. Now it was apparent that he had entered a place of vulnerability while managing the cancer diagnosis. Being present meant acknowledging the past but also embracing the present with a focus on the importance of just being present in the moment with Dad. The ability to be with my Dad and surrender a desire to fix the circumstance was only possible through abiding in Christ. Embracing the power of God that was resident in my own life provided an inner strength of hope, knowing that one day we will be together in heaven.

CHAPTER 4
THEOLOGICAL ANALYSIS OF HOPE

Patterns of hope are wedged like a tapestry in the Messianic philosophy in the neo-Marxist excerpt from Bloch, according to Moltmann, a German theologian. This implies that he is not imitating Bloch nor baptizing it as Karl Bart does. He is simply building a foundation of what his theology of Christianity and Judaism embraces. "The God of promise and exodus, the God who raised Christ and who lets the power of the resurrection dwell in believers is the ground of active and for passive hope" (Moltmann, 1993, p.9). Suffering activates hope. One must be patient and wait through the storms of the difficult seasons of life to become able to minister to others. The primitive root word for hope, *yachal*, means to wait, await, and delay (Strong, p. 49). It has been stated by an unknown poet, "we are going through a storm, coming out of a storm or preparing for a storm in our journey through life." An authentic Christian hope can never be merely lobbed over at others like a brick over a fence. It is born in compassion through community with those who suffer and identify with the wounds of those hurting. Healing and liberation come in unexpected ways. Christian hope is nonetheless unyieldingly confident in the ultimate triumph of compassion over all forms of tyranny, alienation, bondage, and suffering (Stone, 1996).

Ruth, a Moabite daughter-in-law, provided the ministry of presence and hope to Naomi, her mother-in-law, a Jewish widow during a time when her belief system was wavering in hope (Ruth 1:3-5, 16-17). Hope is a real live expectation that your actions communicate what you believe. The secret of Christ in us, the hope of glory, refers to moving forward and walking toward the desired expectation without anxiety (Col 1:27).

In the sixtieth year of Reinhold Neibuhr's career, he experienced the shocking impact of a stroke. It caused his left side to become lame. Having graduated from Yale University, he was a noted theologian, prestigious circuit preacher, and a famous political debater. He was also a sought-after educator that now has found himself in a state of depression and embarrassment after becoming very successful. He reflected upon how the stroke took him to the "sidelines" and reminded him of a prayer that he had written earlier. The prayer was adopted by the Council of Churches and Alcoholic Anonymous organizations: "God give us grace to accept with serenity the things that cannot be changed, courage to change the things that should be changed and the wisdom to distinguish one from the other." Through the stroke and depression, Neibuhr learned more wisdom and compassion for others (McFee-Brown, 1986). Naomi may have felt she was sitting on the "sidelines" of life, serving as a spectator rather than a contributing asset to her family—similar to how Neibuhr described his desire to be actively engaged although he was in a season of anxiety and depression.

The cognitive theory approach to psychology, attempts to explain human behavior by understanding an individual's thought processes. "In cognitive therapy, one's belief systems, or interpretations of the activating event, produces the emotional consequences that one may become depressed. In a family structure, various belief systems are examined. A person may believe that a critical comment is evidence that he or she is totally incompetent, or that everybody should like them and say positive things about them" (Olsen, 1993). In an integrative family assessment, understanding the beliefs and interpretations of family events is central.

Everyone, from time to time, may become depressed and need encouragement.

However, Naomi's worldview implied the Lord's hand had turned against her (Ruth 1:13). She had lost her husband and sons, which represents destitution and famine. Her belief system was based upon the evidence that she is totally unable to support herself or her daughters-in-law (Ruth and Orpah). Naomi's assessment was limited to her interpretation of the future. The ministry of hope that Ruth gave Naomi transcended their individuality, family circumstances, and dynamics. When Naomi hit a wall of hopelessness, Ruth stepped into her world to bring hope. Thereby, reshaping the direction of her life and impacting generations to come.

When Naomi resisted Ruth from following her, Ruth hit a wall (Ruth 1:16-17). The definition of "the wall," represents a place where another layer of transformation occurs and a renewed life of faith begins for those who feel called and have the courage to move into it. The wall represents our will meeting God's will face-to-face. At this point, we decide, if we are willing to surrender and let God direct our lives (Haber & Guelich, 2005). Ruth met God face to face through her decision to follow Naomi rather than abandon her. The process of meeting the wall, which is the specific challenge, required not going underneath it, over it, or around it, but through it, brick by brick. The feelings and healing of each element of our wills will be assessed, as we surrender to God's will. There is a four-phase movement in one's self and toward others. Ruth provided the ministry of presence and hope to Naomi by coming alongside, committing to returning on a journey to Bethlehem, exhibiting faith in a vision, and ultimately seeing the manifestation of the promise, when Boaz—a near kinsman—took Ruth to be his wife (Ruth 4:1-14).

Naomi and Ruth found mercy and favor in the eyes of the Lord with their neighbors in the community of Bethlehem. Boaz—a near kinsman—married Ruth, redeeming their inheritance and restoring their legacy (Ruth 4:13-17).

> And it is indeed true that God may meet us in the neighborhood. But it is crucial for our ministry that we not confuse our relationships with God with our relationship with our neighbors. It is because God first loved us that we can love our neighbor.

Ultimately, it is Christ in us from whom healing comes. Only through Christ can one break through the human alienation and restore the broken connections with each other and God (Nouwen, 1977). Ultimately, God reached out with hope through his servant, Boaz, to extend mercy to Naomi and Ruth.

CHAPTER 5

THEOLOGICAL ANALYSIS OF MERCY

The Hebrew definition of mercy is from the root word "china," and means "beseech, fair, (be, find, shew) favor (able), give, grant (gracious (-lee), entreat, (be) merciful, have (shew) mercy 'on, upon'" (Strong, 1881, p. 41). Christ joins his disciples by coming along side of them during their journey to Emmaus, a time of anxious grieving over the events that led to Christ's death and burial (Luke 24:15). Christ deals with them through the practice of mercy by showing them favor and fairness. He sympathizes with empathy by implementing interpathic in pastoral care. The disciples were facing a crisis in their faith, an imaginable predicament that brought a favorable self-evaluation, blurring their spiritual vision from understanding the mercy of God. Augsburger stated, "Interpathic presence enters another world of human energies and risks, making the self-available to entertain what was formerly alien, to be hospitable to what is utterly new (Augsburger, 1976).

Christ steps into the world of the disciples, listens, and makes himself available to offer mercy—an unmeasurable, undeserved gift of favor. The disciples had abandoned and aborted Christ's mission, and had returned to their regular occupation of fishing (John 21:2). Christ appears to his disciples on the Sea of Galilee and extends an invitation to "feed my sheep." This is an example of "mercy in action." Christ overlooks their faults by extending an olive branch of forgiveness to Peter, Thomas, Nathanael, Zebedee, and two other disciples (John 21:1). Christ has carried all sin and taken on all burdens, yet he also is merciful and compassionate to his disciples by reminding them of their mandate to fulfill the great commission (Col 3:13; Luke 6:36; Matt 28:16-20). Oswald Chambers stated, "Never build forgiveness on the idea that God is our Father and he will forgive us because he loves us." That contradicts the revealed truth of God in Jesus Christ. It makes the cross unnecessary and redemption "much ado about nothing." God forgives sins only because of the death of Christ. God could not forgive people in any other way than by the death of his Son. Jesus is exalted as Savior because of his death. It is because the mercy of God, Jesus Christ hates the sin in people, and Calvary is the measure of that hatred" (Chambers, 1992).

Mercy breeds an unconditional love that allows another to become free of guilt and the impact of condemnation. It also empowers others to invest and utilize their gifts to help others. In the critical journey, Hagberg stated, "I ask God to heal me at a deeper level. One of my greatest healing experiences is being released from resentment and forgiveness of myself and others. I feel gratitude, with a willingness to be about God's healing work in the world. I believe I am, in Henri Nouwen's wise words, a wounded healer" (Hagberg & Guelich, 2005, p.7).

God desires to use every disappointment, hurt and setback to help others be comforted through the comfort that we have received (2 Cor 1:4). Kimball stated, if we were totally helpless, then God would have to do it all for us. Instead we have plenty of choices, lots of freedom, and the power and presence of Jesus Christ. God is living with us to show us how to live. We cannot sit back, then, and ask God to do all the work. We aren't helpless! God won't tolerate us using our humanity as an excuse for not joining him in sharing his power and presence in the world. He has chosen to do his loving through us. (Kimball, 1987, p. 7)

An Old Testament text found in Hosea 6:6, and later highlighted in the New Testament (Matthew 9:13) both contrast a wonderful image of mercy: "I desire mercy not sacrifice." The Old Testament context captures the progressive disobedience of the people of God, because of their idolatry, disobedience, and refusing to honor and obey his statures. God provides a portrait of his unconditional love and mercy for his people.

He allows his prophet Hosea to marry Gomer, a harlot, to serve has an amazing example of his love and mercy for his children. The New Testament is the fulfillment of the Old Testament. Another portrait of love and mercy is found in Matthew 9:13. The Pharisees and Sadducees again mocking Jesus for eating and drinking with the publicans. In the midst of their accusations, Jesus declared; "I have not called the righteous to repentance but the sinner" (Matthew 9:13). The theologian Charles Gerkin stated. "Pastor care is difficult work; caring for individuals, communities including families living together and groups of people who work and play together. There are inevitable tensions involved in providing pastoral care" (Gerkin, 1997, p. 11). Tensions also can reflect as anxiety when those whom one serves are more interested in judgment and sacrifice than walking in mercy and grace. Can you imagine how many persons find it difficult to accept mercy when they have hurt or injured another? Yet God's standard of mercy that he put forth was later demonstrated by allowing his son, Jesus the Christ, to be nailed to the cross for the sins of the world (Rom 5:8).

CHAPTER 6

ROLE OF THE CHURCH FATHERS IN PASTORAL CARE

The church fathers handled the issue of pastoral care in various ways. The term, "fathers in the faith," depicts a rich spiritual heritage of wisdom bestowed upon individuals established in the Christian faith. One of the Nicene and Post-Nicene fathers of the Catholic Church, Gregory the Great, obtained priesthood status through the lineage of his father, St. George. He wrote a treatise referring to pastoral care. Gregory the Great was so humiliated and disgusted that the book was embellished with standards, rituals, and guidelines that no human could ever attain in good conscious. Pastoral care was not clearly understood or comprehended considering what it is today. The piety, greed, and lack of compassion for the poor in the early church is also in the church of the postmodern era. This reminds me of the Pharisees who Apostle Paul served prior to his encounter with the Spirit of God.

After Paul's Damascus Road experience in the New Testament (Acts 9:1-9; 22:611; 26:9-20), which influenced his conversion to Christianity, he describes himself as a "father of the faith" in his New Testament epistle to the Corinthian church (1 Cor 4:15).

God also declares in the Old Testament through the prophets,

> I will open my mouth in a parable; I will utter dark sayings of old: which we have heard and known, and our fathers have told us. We will not hide them from their children, sewing to the generation to

come the praises of the Lord, and his strength, and his wonderful works that he hath done. (Ps 78:2-3)

The term "father" also occurred in Rabbinic Cynic and Pythagorean circles. Early Christian writers such as Clement of Rome, Irenaeus, and Clement of Alexandria all employed the term as one's "instructor." A "father in the faith" is familiar with the teachings concerning the life and ministry of Jesus Christ (Hall, 2002). It is necessary to understand and glean from the history of what our spiritual "fathers of faith" exhibited. Our fathers imparted a spiritual zeal, tremendous theological contribution, and many laid down their life for the faith and were burned at the stake (Hall, 2002).

St. Augustine struggled with his humanity and finally acknowledged that "we are sinners, all saved by grace." He contended for the faith in his City of God writings stating, "The pre-millennialism advocated by other Christian teachers too easily fed their desire for the material rather than spiritual delights and identified the kingdom of God with the church of the world," according to Brian Daley, a noted scholar (Hall, 2002). John Chrysostom, Archbishop of Constantinople in the late fourth century, believed that Jesus' return was imminent and would happen very soon. He advocated that the dangers of an eschatological curiosity should be centered on the gospel. Tertullian, a biblical scholar, believed Jesus chose the twelve disciples and appointed them as leaders of the nation and that the only preaching and doctrine heard in the church should be the apostolic teachings of Christ. We don't have to continue to reinvent the wheel but learn from our traditions and progress in comprehending and communicating spiritual truth. Thomas C. Oden said, "True progress is not change, true progress is an advance in understanding of that which has been fully given is the deposit of the faith" (Oden, 1994).

As stipulated in the Book of Common Prayer, archbishops and bishops are mandated to "preach the gospel of Christ and to heal the sick" (Fox, 1959). Preaching and teaching the gospel also includes administering the word in action by feeding the poor and clothing the naked. An excellent example of how the "Church Fathers" served in pastoral care is found in the early church by the disciples who also fulfilled the office of pastoral care by distributing food to the Grecian widows. The disciples embodied the spirit of Christ through their interpathic servant leadership (Acts 6:1).

Dwight Hopkins, an African American theologian stated, "While whites may have produced the most influential theologians in the Christian tradition, the black church community has produced some of the greatest preachers of the gospel of Jesus. In the nineteenth century, untutored evangelists like Black Harry, Jarena Lee and John Jasper, twentieth–Century orators, like Howard Thurman, and Martin Luther King were powerful role models in pastoral care (Hopkins & Thomas, 2010).

Jesus Christ, the founder and father of the local church demonstrates the importance of the role of pastoral care. He ordained twelve with a purpose to preach, teach, feed the poor, and clothe the naked. He gave them the power to heal sicknesses, diseases, and to cast out devils (Mark 3:14-15; Acts 2:43). "God fulfills his purpose on the earth, through the church, which is a living organism representing his body to empower others" (Jensen, 1999).

CHAPTER 7

THEOLOGY OF MODERN FEMINIST & WOMANIST PERSPECTIVES

Historically, the Jews treated women as property, even as recent as thirty years ago, when women served in various denominations in which male dominance was very apparent. Males dominated the platforms and females served the males in leadership without a voice. A roundtable in the Jewish custom was a symbol of hospitality according to Brita Gill-Austern, a feminist and womanist theologian (Gill-Austern, 2002). She expresses various feminist interpretations and reflections of the roles of women in the church. The connectional principle of discussing perspectives at a roundtable, over a meal, is also a crucial aspect of action and reflection in communities of faith. It correlates to the church's observance of partaking in the communion of the Lord's Supper. The question is, how do we develop a feminist theology about the church that makes sense regarding women's realities and experiences of oppression and yet one that continues to affirm Jesus Christ as the source of life and connection in the church and community? (Russell, 1973).

Most certainly, "feminism" is a modern word, an ideology in the sense of a set of ideas used to bring about social change. Yet the concern to include women, some referred to as marginal persons who have been considered less than human, is not new. Aquino, a Latin feminist stated, "one of the tasks facing women in the sphere of liberating Christian ethics is to criticize and dismantle the foundations of the present socio-religious order, which subordinate's women" (Aquino, 2002, p.187). It is imperative that women continue to strive to demolish the traditional barriers that divide individuals socially which may be grounded in their individualistic perspectives.

The patriarchal framework of our fathers of faith may have placed more emphasis on a woman being subordinate to a man because of their dominating historical paradigms. Often it has been referenced that Apostle Paul supported the position that women should remain silent and not teach in the local church (1 Cor 14:34, 1 Tim 2:12). Women served, particularly in the local church, prior to the twentieth century in various roles of ministry of helps; cooking, cleaning, singing, and working in children's ministries. Women were taught not to usurp authority over a man in the local church. The title of pastoral care, in general, has been dominated prior to the 1960s by male leadership. Today, in many denominational circles it is still distasteful and against church policy for women to become ordained as clergy.

Audre Lorde, an African American poet, published anthologies from her feminism perspective during the 1960s, inspiring women to become transformed from silence, to speak out. It was often articulated to me when serving in a local church that I was too passionate and needed to tone down my zealousness. At the time, having a desire to be accepted and validated caused me to operate in a passive-aggressive posture. After much research and observation, I realized my actions and attitude exhibited a natural leadership.

While most black theology detailed more liberative effects of Jesus' message and ministry for all oppressed people, Black theology initially did not deal with the problem of sexism within the black church. It did not address the problem of emphasizing the manhood or maleness of Jesus. This partly engendered sexist beliefs within the Black church and community (Hopkins, et al., 2010).

It was difficult as a woman to establish a vital strong leadership identity in the church while growing up and hearing about strong male biblical heroes such as Daniel in the lions' den (Dan 6:19-22), Moses' deliverance at the Red Sea (Exo. 14:21), Noah building the ark (Gen 5:32) and David killing Goliath the giant (1 Sam 17:50) were constantly emphasized. Women mentioned such as Deborah the judge, Esther the queen, or Rahab the harlot aided a male leader in his individual vision or assignment from God. Especially in Old Testament accounts of Bible stories, males were depicted as the major and dominant victors. Did you observe any women recognized for their leadership roles by leading the military armies? The twelve disciples, wives, and families travelled with Jesus. A few various names of women were inserted, but not highlighted, in the Old and New Testaments, such as Phoebe, Lydia, and Durcas, to name a few. Some things have not changed but remain the same. As it relates to a favorite Top 10 tune in the 60s, by a famous African American singer, James Brown, "It is a Man's World, but it wouldn't be a thing without a woman or a girl."

In the 1990s, serving as a Baptist missionary in a predominately African American church, it was uncommon for a female chaplain to serve in chaplaincy at the hospitals in Kentucky. It was a shock to see a woman in such a role for the first time. Our family had requested that a male Baptist clergy offer a prayer for my nephew who had been diagnosed with terminal cancer. The hospital sent a female, Catholic chaplain instead. This was the first time our family had been introduced to a female chaplain. The Southern Baptist church had shaped my embedded theological views with limited information regarding women serving in the capacity of pastoral care.

The womanist movement embraces the promotion of self-love vs. self-esteem. Self-esteem happens by empowering people to love themselves and put value on themselves. Women are learning to accept their self-worth and value themselves as having equal abilities to a male. When an oppressed community loves itself, and it values its history, ancestry, land, language, traditions, and its very existence, others will do the same. The womanist movement influences the rights of women to live on earth and develop sacred traditions, value connections with God, relationships, and with all of creation. It is necessary to value ourselves, our bodies, minds and all creation—including our families and extended families—to impact our nation (Hopkins & Thomas, 2010, p. 420).

Women live, work, and play in a society that has always sought to shape and mold them, based upon the media's influence. For instance, in the 1960s, the models on television depicted attractive women as white women with "thin lips." This sent a signal or subliminal message to African American women that to be beautiful one definitely could not have "thick lips." However, in this postmodern era, there is such a melting pot of races depicted on television that anything goes and everyone is beautiful.

Womanist theology is a response to sexism, and Black theology is a response to racism in the feminist theology. When early Black theologians spoke of the Black experience they only included the experiences of Black men and boys. They did not address the unique oppression of black women. Feminist theologians, on the other hand, unwittingly spoke only of a white woman's experiences based predominantly from the middle- and upper-class status quo of white women (Coleman, 2009). Hebrews declares, "today and yesterday is the same for God." Theology often invokes and illustrates how God can shape individuals through his perspectives and transform our personal histories, our past and current contexts for his specific purposes (Coleman, 2008).

An effective post-modernist womanist theologian engages in the activity to educate others by remembering and choosing to teach and honor the heritage of women by communicating individual concrete experiences of the good, bad, and ugly into a context that will produce a creative transformation in our communities to allow for positive interchange between males and females. Coleman stated, "We are not saved apart from our communities in which we participate, for we do not exist for the salvation of our own particular communities. We accept and reciprocate God's love so that we might love ourselves and our neighbors" (Coleman, 2008).

The narrative of Ruth and Naomi portrayed cross cultures and the union of two cultures uniting forces as women who challenged the status quo and shaped the destiny of nations, the eternal lineage of Christ.

CHAPTER 8

THEOLOGY OF PASTORAL CARE ACROSS CULTURES

The gospel message revealed in the Bible urges all who claim the good news for the broken-hearted and the oppressed pursue the mission *dei* to carry forth the mission of God to all far and distant lands on behalf of the liberation of the poor.

Today in Black communities—whether one resides in Africa, Asia, the Caribbean, Latin America, Pacific Islands, or people in Europe or the United States—every person who serves in the capacity as clergy will experience anxiety when practicing pastoral care (Hopkins, Dwight, & Thomas, 2010).

While visiting the country of India, many women are still treated as servants. Many parents continue to serve their traditions by selecting suitable spouses for their children. In the United States this practice would be unacceptable. After visiting various Indian churches, it was clear that practicing pastoral care was based upon their Hindu orthodox practices and family traditions. "The critical task of the church is helping parishioners and counselees discern where the spirit is at work in the lives of their clients. Even if people are aware of God's Spirit component, we cannot assume the pastoral providers have the necessary skills to carry it out" (Wimberly, 1990).

God is at work in every area of our lives. It is important for our leaders to understand and discern the presence of God in our suffering world. Scripture serves to remind pastoral care providers that God is, in the same way, helping our weaknesses, which can be interpreted as our suffering and pains in a fallen world (Rom

Reducing Anxiety of Persons Practicing Pastoral Care

8:26-28). Yet all things do work together for our good and for the glory of God. When we see the anxiety levels of many patients in healthcare communities, it is important to remember we are not alone and only God will aid in dealing with issues in every culture.

In conclusion, this chapter has introduced the historical biblical accounts from the Old and New Testaments that portray biblical characters who overcame the impact of anxiety to practice interpathic pastoral care. For instance, Moses, a father of faith, obtained prudent advice from Jethro, his father-in-law. This allowed him to become successful in administering pastoral care to the Hebrew tribes and families.

Ruth came alongside Naomi, her mother-in-law, to provide comfort and support during a difficult time of grief and famine. This is a hallmark testimony of courage. Both Naomi and Ruth benefited from their partnership; Naomi obtained a family inheritance through the marriage of Ruth to Boaz. Ruth's one act of kindness is an excellent example of interpathic pastoral counsel. Christ on the road to Emmaus with his disciples disclosed the importance of walking through a storm with another until the rainbow is revealed and hope has been restored.

Christ joining his disciples on the road to Emmaus reflects how we are never alone and how our lives will be enriched as we open our eyes to see Christ's influence when others are hurting. Abiding in the relationship with Christ, who is the vine, produces the inner strength to help one reach outside of oneself to a hurting world and bring comfort.

The theological perspectives of the ministry of presence exhibits the incarnation of Christ in an individual. Reaching out and touching another, while journeying with them toward recovery, is a message of hope and mercy. These virtues play a key role in developing the skills to help one move beyond a personal agenda to a place of seeking to help someone in pain. It is imperative that we acknowledge the sacrifices of the "Fathers of faith" who have invested a tremendous heritage that has been given to the church and laid a strong biblical pastoral care foundation through their individual blood, sweat, and tears. Will we pastoral care leaders prepare to do the same through interpathic training?

The theological feminist and womanist perspectives enhance our awareness of the value that women play in our society. Our country has become a melting pot of various races, creeds and colors. Cross-culturally, male and female leaders that reflect the rainbow of colors which were represented in the book of Acts (Acts 2:2). Historically, we can learn to become a reflection of God, and this is conveyed in the Old Testament. We can live out the example of Christ Jesus today and implement the theological perspectives of the ministry of presence, hope and mercy, through a yielded vessel operating in interpathic pastoral care to people who have been assigned to us (John 17).

CHAPTER 9

WHAT IS ANXIETY?

A rose is a beautiful flower. To enjoy its fragrance, persons must handle the rose gently. Each decade is similar to the bud, stem, and thorns of a rose. When practicing pastoral care, one must capture the beauty. "The seventeenth century has been called the Age of Enlightenment, the eighteenth, the Age of Reason; the nineteenth, the Age of Progress; and the twentieth, the Age of Anxiety" (Coleman, 1972, p. 3). This chapter reviews the literature from experts in the field of pastoral care and counseling, defines anxiety, examines statistics relating to anxiety, identifies areas of psychology and anxiety disorders—such as general anxiety disorders (GAD) and posttraumatic stress disorder (PTSD)—methodologies used to access changes in anxiety, my personal experiences of overcoming anxiety, and methodology and ministry approaches that may support reducing anxiety.

Experiencing challenges that may produce some form of anxiety, and which must be managed, is a normal part of life. Webster stated, a state of being uneasy, apprehensive, or worried about what may happen; concern about a possible future event. Psychiatry an abnormal state like this, characterized by a feeling of being powerless and unable to cope with threatening events, typically imaginary, and by physical tension, as shown by sweating, trembling, an eager but often uneasy desire: *anxiety* to do well. (Webster's, 2010)

One must learn to cope properly and defuse an overwhelming sense of worry and anxiety. A person with an anxiety disorder often experiences a significantly reduced quality of life that is unmanageable. Johnson stated,

> Everybody knows that something has happened. Just when it happened, no one knows, but there is a complete agreement that something very important has given way and all sorts of things are pulled out of shape or sagging or falling apart. The result? Nerves! There is a sense of fear as if some impending doom around the next turning in the road. (Johnson, 1951, p. 3)

As a result, persons out of balance experience "a physical cognitive behavior that may be caused by internal or external factors that can trigger anxiety, such as foods, medications or high environmental stimulation and functions to restore balance in all systems" (Wehrenberg, 2008, p. 155). A healthy balance through proper diet, rest, and exercise allows one to cope with an unforeseen crisis that may produce anxiety.

Many people see the lifestyles of rich and famous celebrities as a portrayal of success and ease. For instance, Robin Williams, a famous comedian who was admired and loved, committed suicide. He presented two different personalities, one private and one public. The public one entertained millions with laughter, yet another side struggled with depression, addictions, and chronic anxiety disorders. Chronic anxiety disorders are widespread nationally and abroad: "At least 19 million Americans suffer from anxiety disorders according to research by the National Institute of Mental health" (Davidson, 2003, p. 13). It is a problematic issue. According to the National Institute of Mental Health over 40 million Americans (one of seven) have some kind of anxiety disorder.

The *Journal of American Medical Association* observed anxiety is the most common emotional disorder in countries other than U.S. (Stossel, 2013, p. 9)

"Women normally suffer with more anxiety disorders than men especially in the sixteen to forty-year age group. Anxiety is the primary symptom in 20-25 percent of all psychiatric disorders"

(Seligman, 1990, p. 116). Lim, who conducted research concerning African-Americans, noted:

> African Americans in the general community, as well as those who were diagnosed with depression, had more positive views about seeking mental health care than did their white counterparts. This seems somewhat paradoxical given African Americans were less likely to use mental health services. (Lim, 2006, p. 64)

Although African-Americans are willing to pursue mental health information, some are unwilling to retain mental health professionals.

Although the path to a meaningful life seems to be easy, this generation is obsessed with ambition and obtaining success, which may lead to more stress. This behavior opens a window for more anxiety. Ellis and Joffe-Ellis believe "psychological therapy" is essentially a talking and listening form of help that does not primarily utilize medical or physical means (2011, p.5).

The American Heritage Dictionary defines psychopathology as the "study of the origin, development, and manifestations of mental or behavioral disorders or used to refer to the study of mental disorders. "An individual that may have experienced a failure to communicate effectively or may exhibit an inability be interactive and social with others. Ellis stated,

> Almost all modern authorities in psychology believe that people's estimation of their own value, or worth, is exceptionally important and that they seriously denigrate themselves or have a poor self- image, they will impair their normal functioning and make themselves miserable in many significant ways.

> Consequently, one of the main functions of psychology, is usually held to enhance individuals self- respect (or "ego strength," "self-confidence" or "self-esteem" and "feelings of personal worth." (Ellis, 2005, p.35)

Many psychologists may consider poor self-image as a contribution to one's inability to maintain and suitably function. Greenberg (1989) relates the field of psychotherapy "to the healing of troubled thoughts, feelings, and behaviors that have led to a troubled life" (p. 39). When persons contemplate negative thoughts, a destructive pattern of actions may follow. Craighead, Miklowitz & Craighead stated,

> Psychiatric diagnosis is fundamental to the understanding of mental illness. Without it, the study, assessment and treatment of psychopathology would be disarray. Over 300 diagnoses are housed under the exceedingly umbrella of mental disorder. (Craighead, Miklowitz& Craighead, p.1, 2013)

Craighead, Miklowitz & Craighead (2013) stated "General anxiety disorder (GAD) is a prevalent, chronic debilitating disorder" (p.134). Unfortunately, research on this condition has suffered due to the unreliable and changing diagnostic status of GAD." (p.134). Seligman (1990) stated, that "GAD is a pervasive disorder that affects almost every system of the body" (p. 129).

Every organism is affected by this mental disorder. As a result, persons may become unpredictably anxious. A normal adult will experience panic attacks relating to fear, but various contributing elements enhance GAD. Schoenleber, Chow, and Berenbaum (2014) suggested, "There are several theoretical reasons to expect that self-conscious emotions, in particular, may be associated with worry and GAD" (p.12). Evidence supports a positive association between self-conscious emotional constructs, worry, and GAD.

Bob, a friend from church, describes himself as a "bundle of nerves." For the past month, he had experienced overwhelming anxieties. He fretted because his boss had been concerned, and had questioned him numerous times regarding his work habits. Bob has a track record of being exhausted, reporting late to work, and having an inability to focus and complete work assignments. Bob developed a habit of getting fired from jobs because of regular panic attacks. They drain his energy in every area of his life—at home, at work, and in his friendships. His situation is an example of a person with GAD and mood symptoms, such as "feelings include keyed up, restless, or on edge difficulty concentrating or having one's mind go blank due to worry, disrupted sleep due to worry, muscle tension, irritability and fatigue" (Craighead, Miklowitz, & Craighead, 2013, p. 109). Another anxiety disorder that has impacted the lives of Veterans returning from active military combat is PTSD:

> This condition is known as PTSD went by many names, such as; "traumatic neurosis," "gross stress reaction", "war neurosis," and "combat fatigue." Following the return of thousands of veterans from Vietnam, many of whom exhibited difficulties adjusting back to civilian life, along with the rise of the women's movement, which heightened consciousness of the effects of sexual and physical victimization (e.g., rape trauma syndrome, battered women's syndrome), the modern diagnosis became known as post-traumatic stress disorder. For example, people who believe they will go crazy if they think about the traumatic event will attempt to avoid thoughts about the trauma and will try to keep their mood occupied with other things as much as they can. Someone who believes that he

or she must figure out why this traumatic event happened to keep it from happening again will ruminate about how it could have been prevented. (Craighead et al., 2013, pp. 252–256)

When a traumatic event happens, persons may replay the event to bring understanding and resolution.

Susan, a single, retired Marine veteran, shared countless stories about abandonment and isolation in the field. Now as a civilian, much of her time is spent taking care of her aging mother. She shared in a group that her dad was preparing to relocate, and she again was feeling abandoned. By allowing Susan to share her feelings while listening attentively, she recognized that her feelings were not grounded in her present reality but geared to what happened while serving in the military. Susan's anxiety was reduced, and she was able to regain peace. Facilitating a spirituality group every week as a chaplain employed through the Michael E. DeBakey Medical Administration chaplaincy department in Houston, Texas, the writer had opportunity to work with veterans coping with PTSD syndrome. Cava (2006) stated, "Healing significance of storytelling provides hope and helps those hearing the narrative" (p. 201). For six weeks, the group shared individual narratives, revealing events that had caused tremendous pain and anxiety. As a facilitator, listening and asking meaningful questions allowed them to reframe the events in their lives, brought about a change, and reduced their anxiety level.

Acknowledging chronic symptoms rather than ignoring issues and seeking professional guidance may reduce anxiety. Greenberg (1989) stated, "Some persons may become anxious regarding approaching therapy and may attempt to reassure themselves, cover up the symptoms or just believe their problems will go way" (p. 302). Assessing the client is a part of obtaining necessary information to prepare methodological strategies to access a change in behavior.

Seligman (1990) described a systematic approach to treatment planning by first assessing a client using an instrument he developed, a "client map." It provides an outline of the mental disorder and summarized map of the recommended treatment. "In general, treatment planning moves from the nature of disorder, through consideration of the client's characteristics, to the approach to treatment" (p. 13). In other words, a treatment plan should be detailed and reviewed carefully by the professional and client. Wehrenberg (2008) stated, "It is a powerful tool of healing because some share stories that relieve pain and bring comfort to another that may originate from a brokenness within" (pp. 155–157). Wehrenburg used the following acronyms for his treatment plan: "A" and "B" stand for activating the event and belief system that is held by a person, "C" stands for the consequences, "D" stands for the demands that are placed upon self and others. The narrative is based upon overcoming anxiety through self-talk by setting goals and actions that arise from anxiety.

Persons neglecting to handle negative encounters may experience a greater measure of anxiousness. DiClemente (2006) stated,

> Trans Theoretical Model (TTM), markers of change are signposts that identify where a person stands in two-key change related areas; decision making about change, which is called the decisional balance, and the strength of one's perceived ability to manage the behavior change measured by self-efficacy/temptation status. He suggests four dimensions of change: precomtemplation, contemplation, preparation, action and maintenance based upon the following process. (pp. 24-25)

An article from Whitelaw, Baldwin, Bunton, and Flynn (2000) stated, "It is at least arguable that treatment providers must base their innovations on a sense that something is right and valuable without affording themselves the comfort of waiting for the empirical evidence to totally justify their decisions" (p. 14).

Some treatment plans facilitate an opportunity for personal growth, change, and recovery. TTM treatment is an effective recovery plan to reestablish sound medical health. This model focuses on the decision making of the individual. The core constructs of TTM are the process of change, decision balance, self-efficacy, and overcoming temptation.

Every human being has a measure of anxiety that produces a desire to accomplish a specific goal. The TTM treatment plan also may be adopted in reducing anxiety in a layperson's proficiency to practice pastoral care by incorporating effective steps that intensify the motivation to change by creating a conducive environment for change. This includes setting proper restraints on one's time, maintaining a peaceful presence, and receiving affirmation and compassionate support.

Briefly, in addition to plans discussed, a "Holistic Treatment plan includes a skilled naturopath, practitioner of alternative medicines which may also recommend peppermint or other herbal preparations to calm the patient's digestive tract." Stossel (2013), who was diagnosed with an anxiety disorder, provides a summary of various psychotherapy treatment plans:

> family therapy, group therapy, cognitive behavior therapy (CBT), Rational Emotive behavior therapy (RET), Acceptance and commitment therapy (ACT), Hypnoses, Meditation, Role playing, interceptive, expressive therapy, eye movement, desensitization and repressing (EMDR), self-help work books, massage therapy, prayer, acupuncture, yoga, stoic philosophy and audio tapes. (p. 10)

These methodologies may be used to allow the client to begin a journey and to access change.

Identifying the being and the ending and the meaning of a specific traumatic event in one's past can assist in restoring a balance life. Miller and Baca stated, Quantum change is vivid in a sense that there is an identifiable, distinctive, memorable experience during which transformation occurred or at least began. Quantum process is an effective treatment implementing individual sessions to access and identify unresolved issues. Quantum change are predominately inner transformations, which often occur in the absence of any salient external event. (2001, p. 5) Isn't it amazing that moments in a day may seem like interruptions, but appear clear, recognizable, and concrete, and can change one's entire perspective of a traumatic event?

I experienced the importance of prayer, meditation, and having a specific time when the Spirit of God (Holy Spirit) intervened in a circumstance to restore peace and reduce anxiety. In 2008, Gray, an Asbury Theological Seminary professor, required his students to complete a Christian formation lesson plan. The class was composed of married, middle-class individuals, from various denominations, who practiced pastoral care. My unresolved inner conflict and struggles from overcoming a divorce, feeling inadequate due to a childhood rape, and dropping out of high school triggered the daily panic attacks. These attacks surfaced during student group discussions, about children, family, and interpersonal relationships. When I became overwhelmed emotionally, I took numerous bathroom breaks during class. During public readings of the Christian formation journals and sharing childhood and adulthood narratives, a beam of light flashed within my soul—a moment when the Holy Spirit revealed that all the students in the class shared the same problems and was experiencing the same difficulties. The students were transparent and open when sharing the journals and narratives, which allowed a level of unity and comradery.

Johnson (1989) describing pastoral care through a lay care ministry, said, "The church is a hospital for people that are being prepared to become disciples of Jesus Christ to bring glory and honor to God. Humans are clay vessels being molded that allow their tragedies to become a treasure for another" (p. 22). Obtaining treatment brings balance to one's body and provides coping skills to manage life challenges to produce healing and reduce anxiety triggers and disorders.

A chaplain may not cure sickness or repair wounds, but he or she may relieve anxieties. Chaplains, in relation to assisting veterans in recovery can be useful in relieving anxiety. Williams (1992) stated,

> Regardless of how shallow or deep the veteran's religious convictions are, it appears very productive to provide access to a chaplain early in treatment. The discussion with the chaplain can be general and confined to the concept of guilt vs. sorrow or it may be in depth about to the veteran's concept of sin and religious morality. Whatever the approach used by the chaplain, the feelings of guilt have been expressed and when this is accomplished, one of the major barriers to therapy is reduced. (p. 282)

Hilliard (2005) stated,

Every person is dealing with a deficiency in some area of life, only twenty-five percent of people with anxiety disorders seek professional guidance, and only a fraction receives effective clinical help. Numerous self-help books are emerging to meet a growing need for reliable information about managing anxiety. (p. 16) Self-help books provide a source of information, but never eliminate the need for the advice of a clinical professional practitioner. During one of my clinical pastoral education sessions, another chaplain—while sharing a self-help booklet in class—experienced a panic attack. He was rushed to the hospital due to a chemical deficiency. When the other classmates discovered that he had failed to take his prescribed medications, which resulted in a low blood count, they confronted him in an empathic way, by providing an expectation of hope and encouraging him to build a support system. "Empathy is a prominent factor in promoting positive treatment outcomes; sympathy has an essential role in human relationships. A counselor's awareness of the appropriate use of empathy and sympathy has potential to foster therapeutic gain" (Clark, 2010, p. 100). Interpathy is the ability to implement sympathy and empathy in practice of pastoral care that will reduce a person's anxiety.

Bowen, one of the founding fathers of family therapy, puts great importance upon the concept of the ability to be a non-anxious presence, as referenced in Generation to Generation family systems publication,

> Differentiation means the capacity of a family member to define his or her own life's goals and values apart from surrounding togetherness pressures, to say "1" when others are demanding "you" and "we." It includes the capacity to maintain a (relatively) non anxious presence in the midst of anxious systems, to take maximum responsibility for one's own destiny and emotional being. (Friedman, 1986, p.27)

Bowen suggests, having a non-anxious presence is valuing one's own point of view while being interconnected with others in a family system is a mindset that can reduce personal anxiety in the midst of challenging family matters.

The Wholistic therapy is a similar type of therapeutic plan that can also enhance change in recovery. Anderson (1990) suggested,

> This moralistic approach to treatment adheres to the motive of change that lies within one's self in the form of a "spirit or soul," the self is the will that thinks and feels. The fulfillment of God's promises

is manifested by entering the Kingdom of God is the therapeutic context. (p. 25)

A person's ability to make a choice to change is a derivative of the unconsciousness in one's spirit or soul.

"Sigmund Freud's initial approach to psychoanalysis was to try to bring unconscious contents to the surface beyond the repression barrier so they could be examined and understood" (Gabbard, 2004, p. 3). The following narrative will capture how the unconscious mind can operate. Freud uses the term, "object constancy to refer to the point at which the mother continues to be the most important person for the child regardless of whether she gratifies or frustrates his needs" (Tyson& Tyson, 1990, pp. 131–132). The child's trust in the mother is the most significant factor in life. When a child becomes an adult and the parent dies, the child and parent relationship may be exchanged by developing a relationship with God. Tanksley (2009) stated, "For an individual believer who is struggling with anxiety and the pressures of life, whether directly or indirectly, trusting in God can make a difference" (p. 1). Trusting in God, attending a local church, and connecting with other Christian believers can provide a vital support system.

In summary, after an extensive review of the study of mental disorders relating to GAD, panic attacks, PTSD, and their symptoms has been presented. The case studies, my personal experiences, and methodologies used to access changes in anxiety were clarified in the related literature. Gabbard (2004) provided key concepts of psychodynamic psychotherapy:

> Much of mental life is unconscious, childhood experiences in concert with genetic factors shape the adult, the patient's transference to the therapist is a primary source of understanding, the patient's resistance to the therapy process is a major focus of the therapy, symptoms and behaviors serve multiple

functions and determined by complex and often unconscious forces and a psychodynamic therapist assist the patient in achieving a sense of authenticity and uniqueness. (p. 3)

The mind is like a computer that records the conscious and subconscious events in one's life. What happens during childhood experiences influences the growth and development of every adult. A psychodynamic therapist can offer assistance in persons desiring to overcome an anxiety disorder.

One must choose to draw from his or her own inner strength and accept support from others—pastors, chaplains, psychologists, therapists, and clinicians who can aid in reducing anxiety. A popular proverb says, "It takes a village to raise a child." Johnson (1989) stated, "Through the process of pastoral training, an important aspect of self-sufficiency can be realized as the church community is drawn upon to be a catalyst for healing" (p. 21). The unconditional love from a church community working together implementing sympathy, empathy, and interpathic can reduce anxiety in this nation because "perfect love casts out fear" (1 John 4:18).

CHAPTER 10

METHODOLOGY

The first chapter addressed, "how anxiety can be reduced in practicing pastoral care. Chapter two reviewed scriptures relating to the Old and New Testament case studies demonstrating persons that overcame anxiety through the implementation of interpathic pastoral care. Chapters three through nine, examined biblical, theological, and historical aspects of pastoral care; a theological analysis of mercy and hope; womanist theology; and church fathers' perspectives. Chapter 10 featured methodologies in literature, describing the various types of anxiety disorders and symptoms, and methodologies that can be used to access change, and that may heighten one's anxiety physically, sociologically, and physiologically. Interpathic pastoral care training will reduce anxiety and empower persons to practice pastoral care through a process of compassionately applying sympathy and empathy in addressing the needs of patients.

This chapter outlines objectives, rationale, procedure, and materials used to conduct the interpathic pastoral training research.

The objective of this book was to determine if persons practicing pastoral care can integrate and facilitate interpathic pastoral care in one's daily routine, and can an interpathic teaching series assist laypersons in reducing anxiety and a reluctance to practice personal pastoral care. The methods used will be qualitative and quantitative by utilizing instruments, such as an application (to review background), demographic survey assessment, and questionnaire instruments. The application and demographic assessment survey gathered a pool of interested pastoral care persons to ascertain and define their level of anxiety in practicing personal pastoral care. The demographic survey documented the feasibility for implementing an interpathic pastoral care training program in the local church. Hagberg and Guelich (2004) suggested, "In seasons of ministry, dealing with personal doubts and fear, it is vital for laypersons to become equipped in helping others and to embrace the optimum meaning of suitable pastoral care" (p. 15). Interpathic pastoral care includes setting proper restraints on one's time, supplying ministry without anxiousness present, and graciously providing a compassionate ear. Everyone encounters a certain measure of anxiety in the daily challenges and routines of life. When factors that produce, anxiety are identified and defused, practicing pastoral care will become more effective.

The third chapter evaluated common assumptions among clergy that impact the ability to administer personal pastoral care to another. Defining anxiety disorders and symptoms, and various research treatment methods and techniques about overcoming one's anxiety were identified. Data will be gathered from the following assessments: A pre-competence survey will review one's present level of anxiety and the post competence assessment will determine when, and if, a participant's anxiety was lessened after eight training sessions.

To reduce anxiety in persons practicing pastoral care in the local church, a method of training included an eight-week series of interpathic pastoral care: Christian Formation I & II, Six Stages of Journey of Faith, Abiding in the Vine, Sympathy, Empathy and Compassion, Trio-Logical Process, and Application of the Narrative Story. This training is designed to prepare one to enter the world of another and implement practical interpathic pastoral care.

The rationale was to reduce the effects of anxiety in laypersons that may cause limitations in practicing personal pastoral care. This training would be of tremendous value to local pastors and leaders in training ministers of the gospel. When persons are trained properly in interpathic personal pastoral care, they give those residing in their communities a witness, acknowledging the presence of the unconditional love found in Christ. Once believers overcome their anxiety and reluctance to practice personal pastoral care with others, a positive attitude in laypersons toward witnessing the love of Christ will give way to increased caregivers, thereby equipping laypersons to provide interpathic pastoral care that strengthens laity and undergirds the local pastor.

The interpathic assessment identified the specific causes of an individual's anxiety to administer pastoral care to others. This training program also will motivate believers to overcome their anxiety and reluctance to practice personal pastoral care with others. The training will be a powerful tool that also will support the mission and vision of any local church. It activates the love of Christ, the congregation, and community.

The survey and research implemented at Hope Church Pearland, Pearland, Texas, was executed by the consultants from Branches Inc. The research sample represented twenty-five laity and minister's members of the congregation from Hope Church Pearland. The training was in eight sessions conducted on Saturdays for four weeks, from 9:00 a.m. through 12:00 p.m. A marketing flyer was distributed to prospective participants four to five weeks prior to the beginning of the sessions (see Appendix A). Demographic information of the target group participating (Appendix B), the interpathic training application (see Appendix C). The training course outline focused on the 25 target participants, components, and duration of training (see Appendix D). The pre- and post-test assessment surveys (see Appendix E). Eight topical training syllabi and outlines for administering the training (see Appendices F–L). An attendance sheet for participants (see Appendix M). A certificate reflecting the completion of the eight sessions (see Appendix N). A word of exhortation to the graduating students (see Appendix O).

Laypersons and/or practitioners identified their ministerial calling, learned how to implement their spiritual giftedness, and understand and walk in spiritual discernment while administering personal pastoral care to others during times of crisis. Through interpathic pastoral training, the participants became reassured in their specific role as personal pastoral caregivers, thereby becoming more supportive of the pastor in their local church and enhancing the local church's outreach ministry.

The pre- and post-test assessment, initial survey, and application provided demographic data for the 25 participants. The information for the participants included their age and gender. The demographic survey also ascertains the denomination and educational backgrounds of the participants entering pastoral care (see Appendix B).

The pre-test assessment survey reflected the individual's level of anxiety prior to training. The same questions in the pre-test and in the post-test, determine an individual's level of anxiety after the interpathic pastoral care training sessions.

Wehrenberg (2008) stated,

Anxiety symptoms are usually not happening because of any real risk. It may be biochemical as panic, worry and social fears. The biochemical process can be changed by changing thoughts and behaviors. Changing one's self-talk is a key component of changing behavior (beliefs, drive, and action). Practicing new behavior is the ultimate way to change the anxious brain. (p. 153) During the training sessions, the facilitators conducted self-talk exercises with the participants. A post-competence assessment survey was administered after the pastoral care training to evaluate if a participant's anxiety level has lessened (see Appendix E).

In summary, laity developed skills in how to ask meaningful questions, and exegete persons, situations, and context when ministering to the wounded person during a time of crisis (see Appendices). Laity acquired guidance in administering personal pastoral care to bereaved families, the sick, and persons who are homebound (shut-in). The participants matured and gain valuable knowledge in understanding the differences between sympathy, empathy, and interpathic pastoral care. The Gospel of Matthew declares the importance of these core values in discipleship in seeking to become obedient to the Great Commission given to the church (Matt 28:19-20). Williams (2003) stated: Faith in God separates the theologian who provides pastoral care and counseling from those care givers who bare their practice of care for others on scientific principles. Faith in God, even with doubts, uncertainties, despair and struggles, is primary and necessary for effective pastoral care and counseling, according to Williams (p. 35).

Finally, Branches Inc. team facilitators analyzed the research project results, and findings, submitted to data to the participants and pastor of the church. An appreciation celebration was conducted for the participants with a certificate of completion, exhortation prayer from Rev. W.C. Smith was presented to participants to conclude the research project. Appendices F–P =include the materials used to conduct the interpathic pastoral training sessions.

CHAPTER 11

INTERPATHIC TRAINING ASSESSMENT SURVEY POPULATION SAMPLE

The project had two objectives. The first, determining if persons practicing pastoral care integrate interpathic training to facilitate interpathic pastoral care into one's daily routine. The second, to ascertain if teaching participants a series relating to Christian formation, critical journey (hitting the walls), abiding in the vine, trio-logical process, and application of narrative story reduces anxiety.

When the anxiety level is reduced of those desiring to practice pastoral care at Hope Church Pearland, Texas the participants will implement their pastoral care skills in the local church. The participants will become an extension of the love of Christ and a witness to those of the community that will touch a hurting society with the healing power of Christ through interpathic pastoral care.

The Assessment Survey Questionnaire and Population Sample included the following stipulations: 25 African-American persons practicing or desiring to practice pastoral care at Hope Church Pearland, Texas. Although Hope Church has a large male population, women made up the largest group of the participants. The demographics of the interpathic research participants were as follows: 80% female, 20% male, 60% married, 32% single, 4% divorced, and 1% widowed.

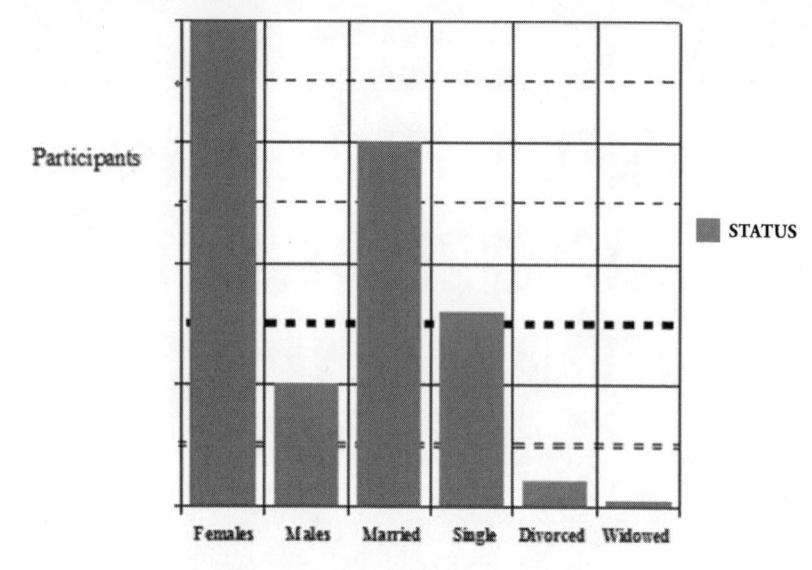

Figure 1. Demographic Status Chart

Of the 25 participants, 16 % were serving in some capacity in pastoral care, 32% were military, 36% worked in the corporate, 4% in industrial settings, 4% in farming, and 8% other (non-disclosure: (see Figure 2). Age is not appearing to be a factor in participants desiring to practice pastoral care at Hope Church. Elders are still very much involved in the local church (see Table 1).

Table 1. Age of Participants and Pastoral Care Activity in Church

Years of Age	n	%
25-44	2	8
45-64	14	56
67-74	8	43
75 and over	1	4

Reducing Anxiety of Persons Practicing Pastoral Care

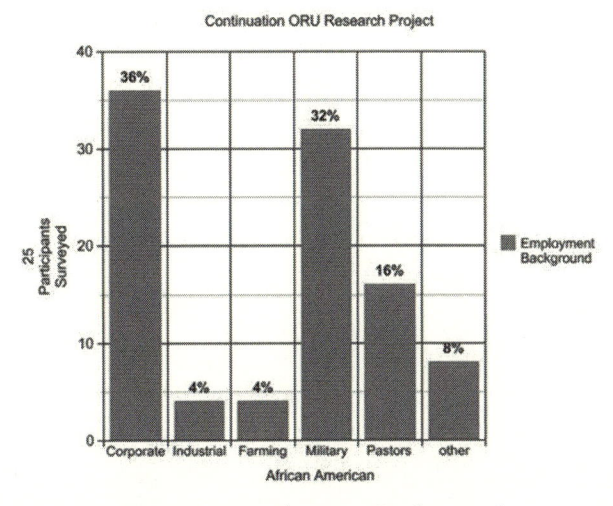

Figure 2. Employment Background

The participants were from the following various denominational backgrounds, reflecting a high range of United Methodist parishioners serving, followed by Baptist (see Table 2).

Table 2. Denominational Backgrounds

Denomination	n
Baptist	7
Methodist	11
Pentecostal	5
Church of God	1
Presbyterian	1

The participants' length of membership breakdown show that they remain faithful at a high rate (see Figure 3).

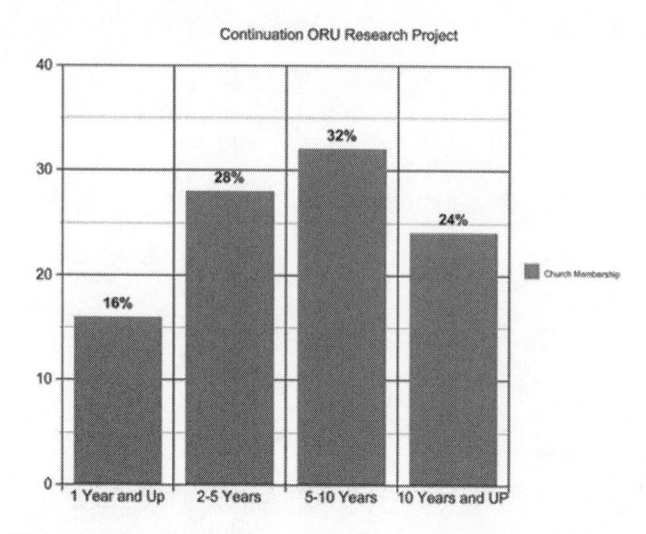

Figure 3. Church Membership at Hope Church Pearland, Texas

The participants at Hope Church reflected a highly-educated base. These figures may be contributed to the pastor and first lady also being highly educated (see Figure 4).

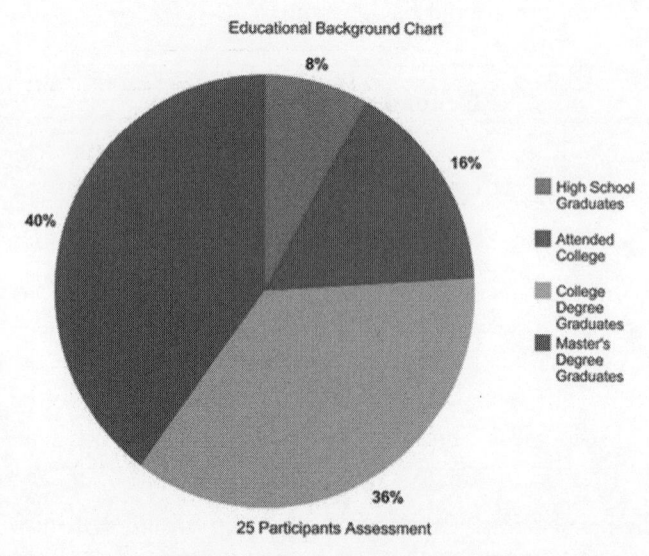

Figure 4. Educational Background

Table 3 indicates the most frequent demographic categories among the participants.

Table 3. Top Results by Demographic Category

Demographic	Top Category	%
Age	45-64	44
Education	College degree	36
Length of church Membership	5-10 years attending the same church	32
Occupation	Corporate sector	36
Denomination	Methodist	11
Gender	Female	80
Marital status	Currently married	60

Table 4 provides the 10-question survey results and the changes, positive and negative, for each question following the intervention. The questions relate to anxiety, its symptoms are based upon the summary conveyed in Chapter 4 and lay leaders were taught how to discern situations presented in pastoral care. A post assessment survey was given after the participants developed a Christian formation timeline and experienced the comprehensive eight interpathic pastoral care training sessions. The Christian formation sessions one and two required the participants to develop their own timeline of events, encounters, and experiences from birth to adulthood. Techniques were taught and the participants recognized from their own experiences how anxiety can be understood through the Christian formation process of examining life events and learning to reframe their past encounters with positive applications. Questions concerning the participants' responses revealed some interesting information reflected in Table 5. The questions related to the summary conveyed in Chapter Four regarding participants' ability to discern situations in the context of a pastoral care setting. The difference between the pre-assessment and the post-assessment results indicate a lowering of participants' anxiety in several situations while gaining confidence in their pastoral care.

Table 4. Survey Provides 10 Question Survey Results

	Questions	Pre-survey		Post-survey		Change
		Yes %	No %	Yes %	No %	%
*1.	Do I hesitate when I introduce myself to others?	28	72	4	96	24
*2.	Do I give eye contact when listening to another?	76	24	80	20	4
3.	Do I greet strangers?	60	40	76	24	16
4.	Is it easy to welcome others into a conversation?	44	56	80	20	36
5.	Do I resist speaking to a group?	40	52	32	68	16
6.	Is it easier to speak one on one rather than to a group?	56	44	44	56	12

*7.	Are you afraid to express how you feel?	52	48	28	72	24
8.	Do I perspire when asked to do a new project?	56	44	40	60	16
9.	Do I perspire when asked to do a new project?	56	44	24	72	28
10.	I believe in drawing strength from a higher power?	100	Nil	100	Nil	Nil

Table 5. Female/Male Results from Questions 1, 2, 7.

	Females		Males	
	Yes %	No %	Yes %	No %
Survey	Pre	Post	Pre	Post
*Q #1	61	39	10	90
*Q #2	73	27	61	39
*Q #7	82	18	30	70

Results of Question #1 Women and Men reduced anxiety according to post-survey.

#2 Women and Men reduced anxiety according to post survey.

#7 Women and Men had reduced fear according to post survey.

Table 6. Employment/Occupation Question Results

	Corporate		Industrial		Military		Pastors		Other	
	Pre%	Post%	Pre%	Post%	Pre%	Post%	Pre%	Post%	Pre%	Post%
	Yes	No	Yes	No	Yes	No	Yes	No	Yes	No
*Q#1	19	32	34	06	15	26	10	33	22	03
*Q#2	22	29	09	12	28	28	30	30	04	01
*Q#7	28	31	31	34	17	21	18	08	06	06

Q#1, 2, 7 Industrial and Military experienced the highest7AS+ reduction in anxiety after the post survey.

Table 7. Denomination Survey Question Results

	Baptist		Methodist		Pentecosatal		Church of God		Presbyterian	
	Pre%	Post%	Pre%	Post%	Pre%	Post%	Pre%	Post%	Pre%	Post%
	Yes	No	Yes	No	Yes	No	Yes	No	Yes	No
*Q#1	18	19	24	25	21	22	22	23	15	11
*Q#2	19	21	25	26	20	21	19	20	17	12
*Q#7	21	22	22	23	19	20	18	19	20	16

Q # 1, 2, 7 Methodist experienced the highest reduction in anxiety.

Table 8. Educational Survey Question Results

	High School		Attended College		College Degree		Master's/ Graduates	
	Pre%	Post%	Pre%	Post%	Pre%	Post%	Pre%	Post%
	Yes	No	Yes	No	Yes	No	Yes	No
*Q#1	18	19	24	25	21	22	15	11
*Q#2	19	21	25	26	20	21	17	12
*Q#7	21	22	22	23	19	20	20	16

Q # 1, 2, 7 High School and Some College experienced the highest reduction in anxiety.

In summary, each participant had an opportunity to process and share his or her own personal narrative and story, understand the importance of identifying any agonic moment in his or her Christian formation that represented a moment of interconnection with God and that brought about understanding of his divine destiny in achieving interpathic pastoral care. Learning the difference between empathy, sympathy, compassion, and the administration of each element as needed in pastoral care. Presenting the same questions to the participants for the pre- and post-assessment provided a measure of evaluating one's anxiety level before and after the training. Many participants after the training have volunteered to serve in various pastoral care roles in the church.

During the post-assessment, the same questions were submitted for their response. The pre-assessment may have revealed in many cases a higher level of withdrawing from the situation/opportunity proposed. However, in the post-assessment, scores reflect the participants' positive change in introducing oneself to others, speaking to a group, not being afraid to share one's feelings, or approaching a new project.

The following are comments made from the participants after the interpathic pastoral care training:

1. "I was able to reduce anxiety and learned how to deal with pastoral care issues."
2. "My anxiety level has been lessened and now I am able to confront concerns that in the past I had trouble in addressing."
3. "I am able to now volunteer in the church because my anxiety was reduced following the training sessions and to begin new projects."

4. "I am able to volunteer with the altar guild and the anxiety to speak to others has lessened."
5. "After hearing the session on sharing one's story and narrative, I am now able to share my story with others because the anxiety has been reduced and fear removed."
6. "During the Christian Formation, I & II sessions I was able for the first time to share a painful event that happened in my life. I am able to also sing in the public again because the fear of singing was lifted and the anxiety reduced.
7. "As I implemented and applied the precepts from the training sessions I was able to gage a reduced anxiety level during my post-assessment that was significantly different from the pre-assessment."
8. "The "Critical Journey" sessions identified how I hit a wall that was paralyzing. I can now work through difficult circumstances rather than focusing on how I feel. Negative thoughts produce negative feelings which can heighten anxiety. My anxiety was reduced during the understanding that I can draw upon a higher power than myself to help me to walk in peace."

Based upon the evidence from the participant's comments relating to the eight training sessions, anxiety and barriers were reduced. When the participants understood, and processed the training series their approach to pastoral care was replaced with confidence to practice pastoral care more effectively.

The following research project questions were addresses: (1) Can persons practicing pastoral care integrate interpathic training to facilitate interpathic pastoral care into one's daily routine? (2) Can a teaching series relating to Christian formation, critical journey (hitting the walls), abiding in the vine, trio-logical process, and application of narrative story reduce anxiety?

CHAPTER 12

INTERPRETATION & RESPONSE & FINDINGS

"Reducing Anxiety of Persons Practicing Pastoral Care through Interpathic Training" research provided useful information. The interpretation, response and findings of the research was based upon the following: assessment survey questionnaire, demographic status chart, employment background chart, participants (pastors and laypersons), age range chart, denominational background chart, church membership chart, educational background chart, pre- and post-survey chart with explanation concerning the participant's response and explanation of the questions from the research data. The interpretation of the results and objections, including the data gathered from conclusions, theological reflections, recommendations, an overview of Chapters one through eleven with a summary of the research comprise the content of this chapter.

The results of this study were given to twenty-five African-American persons practicing or desiring to practice pastoral care, 80% of whom were women and 20% of whom were men. A probable cause for the anxiety some women experience when desiring to practice pastoral care may be suggested from the patriarchal spiritual historical paradigms of the fathers of faith, biblical interpretation of placing more emphasis on women being subordinate to men based upon the Apostle Paul's writings referenced from Scripture (1 Cor 14:34; 1 Tim 2:12), and a field of pastoral caregivers

that was dominated by male leadership prior to the 1960's. Women were taught not to usurp authority over men in the local church; however, once women begin to practice pastoral care, they may experience anxiety, thinking they are usurping authority over men. A careful interpretation of the scriptural prohibitions regarding *usurping authority* would have eliminated such anxiety. Burke (2011) addresses this concern:

> We were led to believe that feminists were a negative influence on our society and to be avoided at all cost, not realizing what was happening to the men's and women's roles. Consequently, many did not change at all, and those that did experienced much confusion and pain brought about by being the first women to challenge the narrow interpretation of women's roles in the home and church. (p. 111)

Women may have experienced discouragement to acknowledge a pastoral role, due to the misconceived perceptions of society regarding the male and female roles in the local church. Review of the literature in chapter two regarding the feminist theological perspectives affirms that women have enhanced the field of pastoral care and played a valuable role in American society. The demographic status chart confirmed more females are entering the field of pastoral care than males. This chart indicates that of those entering ministry, 60% are married couples and 32% are singles. Kennedy (2003) stated,

> Cooper-White outlines several ways in which male clergy enjoy a significant power differential with respect to their female constituents. There is the spiritual authority of the "man of God" role; there is the notion of male authority (men as protectors and sexual dominators) and the authority of the teacher or counseling role ostensibly based on advanced wisdom and experience. (p. 226)

Unfortunately, women in ministry have been mistreated while seeking to serve. A friend attended a church shortly after her divorce. The pastor made unethical and inappropriate advances. In an attempt to cover up the illicit actions, he began to defame this new member's name. Shortly, thereafter, the person left the church.

Hamman (2010) stated,

> Of the challenges facing women clergy, one of the most frustrating has been the growing backlash against their presence in many religious organizations, as much through passive occupational restructuring as through overt resistance, the percentage for clergywomen decreased from 81% to 72%, while the percentages for men were 59% in 1980–1981 and 46% in 1993–1994. (p. 771)

This narrative is not far removed from the narratives that many clergywomen have shared in private regarding personal encounters while practicing pastoral care. The findings in the sampling chart indicate that 80% married women to 32% single women participants took the research.

The employment background chart indicates a very important fact: 36% of persons practicing pastoral care are involved in corporate society. These members are ranked highest participants in church leadership. In addition, many participants fell into the age bracket from 65 to 74 (eight) in comparison to the age bracket of ages 45 to 64 (two), and the lowest number of participants in the age bracket of 75 and over (two).

Pearland Texas Economic Development Corporation Demographic Findings (2013) regarding residents: "professional degrees; 16.8% compared to the U.S. figure of 11.2% and those attaining a Bachelor's degree or higher 46.0% compared to the U.S. figure of 29.6%." Pearland's residents rank higher in education compared to the national average according to the statistical data.

Results seem to indicate that baby boomers (age range of 52 to 60) ranked higher in church membership and attendance at Hope Church Pearland. The baby boomers are those born at the end of World War II or more expressly during 1946 to 1964. Anderson (1994) stated,

The baby boomers returning to church have been dubbed "baby boomerangs." Most of them grew up in religious households. In fact, about 96 percent had some religious instruction in their early years. But many jettisoned their religious beliefs when they became adults because spirituality seemed irrelevant in the secular, pluralistic culture of modern life. Now, like boomerangs return to the point of their departure, many baby boomers are returning to church. The Boomerangs generation are those that were baby boomers in their formative years and may have been disillusioned with the local church and have decided to return to their early beginnings.

The research data indicates that many of the participants have retired from corporate jobs and are presently embracing pastoral care as a second career. In describing the church backgrounds of participants, the data reflects that 44% of the participants were United Methodist, followed by 28% Baptist, and 20% Pentecostal. Although it was surprising that data reflected such a high ratio from United Methodist congregations, the participants' breakdown represents the members of the church being faithful. In the mainline denomination 32% remain committed to attending church, which includes the United Methodists. Barna Research Group (2008) stated,

> Adults who had attended a conventional church (i.e., a congregational-style, local church) during the past month had not attended a house church. Almost three out of every five adults (56%) fit this description. This participation includes attending any of a wide variety of conventional-church events,

such as weekend services, mid-week services, special events, or church-based classes.

Persons remaining faithful to spiritual practices by attending church experience reduced anxiety. Another positive variable indicated from the research project reflected the educational background of the 25 participants, indicating a high academic standard, 36% were college graduates with 40% of the participants holding master's degrees. These findings indicate the influence of the pastoral leadership staff model of Hope Church Pearland, mainly the pastor and his wife. Both have obtained Master's and doctoral degrees.

The more knowledge that one acquires relating to the study of pastoral care, the less anxiety may be experienced in practicing pastoral care. The interpathic training sessions exposed the participants to more information regarding pastoral care. As a result, the participants' anxiety levels were reduced significantly, and they began to volunteer in pastoral care areas in the local church.

The first objective of the research project was to determine if persons practicing pastoral care will be able to integrate and facilitate interpathic pastoral care in a daily routine. The second objective was to ascertain whether a teaching series relating to Christian formation, critical journey (hitting the wall) abiding in the vine, trio-logical process and application of a narrative story reduce anxiety. The data in the pre- and post-survey questionnaires determine if the training was effective in reducing the anxiety of the participants practicing pastoral care after the training series. The first objective was to invite the twenty-five participants surveyed to consider integrating interpathic pastoral care by volunteering in the local church and administering pastoral care in various areas of the church as they were empowered to do so after the training.

The research findings seem to indicate that the participants' anxiety levels were reduced through the responses from the pretest in comparison to the posttest questions (see Table 5). In response to the first question of the pre-survey, seven of the 25 applicants responded *yes* to the question, "Do I hesitate when I introduce myself to others?" After completing the eight sessions of interpathic pastoral care training, the participants' post-survey anxiety was very much lessened with 24 of 25 responding *no* to the same question. After the training the participants' anxiety was reduced significantly, and they immediately volunteered to serve in pastoral care areas of the local church.

The fourth question in the pre-survey indicated 44% of participants responded *yes* while 56% responded *no* to the question, "Is it easy to welcome others into a conversation?" In the post-survey participants responded 80% *yes* and 20% responded *no* to this question. Nine participants who had been anxious about welcoming others into a conversation now found doing so easy, indicating the training was very effective in reducing anxiety in this area.

Responses to question number seven also denote a reduction of anxiety when comparing the participants' pre- and posttest responses. To the seventh question, "Am I afraid to express how I feel?" 13 participants responded *yes* and 12 *no*, reveal a difference of only one respondent. However, the post-survey signifies seven *yes* responses and 18 *no* responses, reflect an increase of 24% in the number of participants who were no longer afraid to express how they feel. Reducing anxiety gave more participants confidence to move beyond themselves, which was also confirmed by the Christian formation timeline constructed by each student.

As implied, the participants' anxiety was effectively reduced after the conclusion of the series of interpathic training. The participants were also able to intergrate the training into daily routines by immediately volunteering in pastoral care at the church. Prior to training, 90% of the participants surveyed were not involved in the pastoral care role of the church. The training was helpful because it provided a platform and method of assessment so that the pastoral staff was better equipped to assist in leadership development of the participants to serve in Hope Church Pearland. After the training, participants were able to engage in outreach and extend the capacity of the arms of the pastoral staff in the church and community.

The research project reiterates an essential benefit for persons practicing pastoral care to obtain support and camaraderie while exercising pastoral care. This evidence was indicated by the response of the participants positively to the Branches, Inc., team facilitators. The participants respected, cherished, and welcomed the facilitators of the eight sessions of interpathic pastoral care. The facilitators were available to address questions and concerns that relate to reducing the anxiety of the participants. The participants applied the principles of Christian formation and critical journey by using materials and exercises that pinpointed areas hindering spiritual growth and development in effectively administering pastoral care to others.

Clebsch and Jaekle (1964), leaders in religious studies, stated, "The sustaining function of the cure of souls in our day continues to be a crucially important ministry" (p. 81). The Branches Inc., team reduced anxiety and prevented possible pastoral care practitioner causalities by imparting their time, energy, and efforts in the training sessions. Anxiety was reduced when facilitators identified factors that stifled the spiritual growth of participants. Persons were experiencing anxiety due to their inability to process events that reinforced anxiety and apprehension, thereby preventing progress. Once the trauma was recognized, shared, and reframed from a negative encounter to a positive memory, the anxiety was reduced. For the first time following the event, the participants could share their narrative encounters publicly, which aided in the ability of other participants to move beyond their traumas to practice pastoral care. This interchange between facilitators and students was the vehicle that reduced anxiety in the participants and produced healing to their souls. Scriptures compare the sharpening of an iron object to the ability that a person has by enlightening another through exchange of experiences in dialogues between individuals (Prov 27:17). The dialogue in the training sessions, including the questions and comments processed and the shared experience by the facilitators and participants were as irons that sharpen one another. As a result of the interpathic training, the team members have become more empowered to teach and began scheduling interpathic training seminars in local churches across the country.

The research had several problems that prevented it from being statistically helpful in determining the effectiveness of interpathic pastoral care training for laypersons and clergy. First, research was conducted with a sample of only 25 participants. A larger sample of laypersons and clergy in other churches and denominations rather than one church and denomination is needed to receive more significant results.

Second, the data was limited to the demographic revealed in the participants whose background was only from the United Methodist, Baptist, Pentecostal, Church of God, and Presbyterian denominations in Pearland. The research data findings might have been different from other church memberships and various geographical areas. The results may have been different as they relate to other cultures since Hope Church Pearland is predominately African American. Research suggests the need for facilitators from seminaries and other arenas of pastoral care training to generate more research data in the arena of interpathic pastoral care materials. Emmanuel (2013) stated,

> Research in palliative care, noted Emanuel, has covered such subjects as the physiology of pain, social science and philosophy of advance care planning, and the withdrawal and withholding of life sustaining treatment. It has looked at physical symptoms of fatigue, nausea, loss of appetite, breathlessness, depression and anxiety. What's missing, is the spiritual care research, there is no

data yet in medicine. In other words, there seems to be limited and inadequate research in the area of spiritual care compared to other healthcare research topics of study.

CHAPTER 13

THEOLOGICAL REFLECTIONS

However, based upon the research of Interpathic Pastoral Care Training does equip, mobilize, support and strengthen memberships in local churches. The pastor of the local church will be enabled to focus on other critical areas of the church, and constructive methods will be implemented to minister to more people.

The embedded theological perspectives of the participants were reconstructed from Old and New Testament case studies referenced in chapter two:

- An elder father-in-law (Jethro) assisting his son-in-law (Moses), reducing anxiety and bringing deliverance by providing an effective method of interpathic pastoral care through delegation (Exo. 18:18, 19-24);
- Ruth and Naomi when Ruth comforted Naomi as they journeyed to Judah and restoration came to Naomi through Ruth's relationship with Boaz (Ruth 1:6-22);
- Disciples on the road to Emmaus being perplexed regarding the events surrounding the crucifixion, death, and burial of Christ when during their dilemma, Christ, their mentor, appeared on the road with them and began to clarify the events so that suddenly their eyes were open and their anxieties were reduced (Luke 24:13).

Anxieties can be reduced and apprehensiveness released through a relationship with a mentor. Opening one's self to the gift of transparency when all anxiety and fear is replaced with confidence and peace is the goal of a mentoring relationship.

The participants confessed scriptures used as a foundation for prayer to reducing anxiety, such as, "Perfect love casts out fear, because fear has torment" (John 4:18); and, "don't be anxious about anything but in every situation by prayer and petition with thanksgiving, present your requests to God and the peace of God which transcends all understanding, will guard your hearts and your minds in Christ Jesus" (Phil 4:6-7). Participants meditated on the Word in every session and experienced a release as their anxieties and fears dissipated through the influence of the mentors/facilitators, training materials, and biblical teachings.

Carvalho, Lopes, Hollanda, Prado, Marciano, & Braga (2014) stated, "The act of prayer is a frequent spiritual activity that promotes well-being, facilitates the health illness process and offers health benefits."

Prayer and meditating on scriptures are an act of communion in abiding in Christ. The theological implication of abiding in Christ was also demonstrated when Christ humbled Himself by demonstrating His love for humanity during His birth, death, and resurrection (John 3:16-17). The participants also humbled themselves by taking time from families, work, and recreation to become trained as a way of extending their love to others. Paul references the methodology of Christ's example of humility. He decreased Himself and accomplished the goals and objectives of His Father through obtaining His empowerment and strength from God (1 Cor 4:6-16; 2 Thess 3:7). The importance of spiritual disciplines such as worship, scripture reading, meditation, and prayer reduce anxiety in those desiring to practice pastoral care by abiding in the vine (John 15:5).

The 25 participants of the research were open to receive counsel and to maintain spiritual practices. Reducing anxiety was accomplished also by providing information and encouragement to those who participated in the research. Areas of weakness within the participants that were hidden from natural lenses were revealed through the transparency of the facilitators and by participants reading the Christian formation pilgrimages, hearing the narratives brought an awareness that the tragedies in their journey worked out for their good and spiritual growth. Science now provides support for the biblical perspectives that indicate stress, which produces anxiety, can be reduced significantly by changing thought patterns. Accordingly, Perts (1997) stated, There is a bio molecular basis for our emotions that establish the crucial healing link between the mind and body. Approximately, 87% of illnesses can be attributed to our thought life, 13% to our diet, and 5% to genetics and environment. (p. 325)

These studies link more chronic diseases to an epidemic of toxic emotions that emerge from the thought patterns in our brain that can produce stress and cause anxiety.

Research compiled by author C. Leaf (2007) stated,

> When you think good thoughts, your brain releases some feel-good chemicals called Endorphins in response to those happy emotions. When you think bad or negative thoughts your brain releases some, I feel bad toxic chemicals called cortisol in response to those negative emotions which can produce stress or anxiety. (pp. 17–18)

In other words, a brain can be compared to a prolific factory producing a variety of chemicals, depending upon what type of emotions one is experiencing.

Nouwen (1982) a theologian, provides the following theological perspective that encompasses the heart of pastoral care:

> And it is indeed true that God may meet us in the neighbor. But it is crucial for our ministry that we not confuse our relationships with God with our relationship with our neighbors. It is because God first loved us that we can love our neighbor.

> Ultimately, it is Christ in us from whom healing comes. Only Christ can break through our human alienation and restore the broken connections with each other and God. (p. 5)

The training sessions produced a deeper depth of spiritual maturity that may never be scientifically measured. However, the data from the 25-student sampling reflects a reduced measure of anxiety. From the examination of the data, a confirmation of success from the 25 students trained and the comments in Chapter 5 from the students indicate that the research was effective in reducing anxiety and the training was beneficial. It allowed participants to break free from human barriers and to restore interpersonal relationships between leaders and peers through the facilitation of the sessions. The narratives helped the participants to reframe negative thoughts and behaviors from previous events.

In summary, this research has revealed an aspect of pastoral care often overlooked. One of the most valuable methods of research was obtaining an awareness of how individual participants' and the facilitator's spiritual giftedness evolved from the beginning to the conclusion of the sessions.

Personally, experiences in various venues, denominations, and churches, serving with pastors, teachers, evangelists, apostles, and prophets, have afforded me the opportunity to explore and understand the true meaning of interpathic pastoral care training. I remember a season when my mother was serving as a pastor's wife. To my surprise, she felt alone and isolated in ministry most of the time. McMinn (2005) stated, in one survey 56% of clergy wives reported having no close friends, and one-fifth of the women believed that people shy away from them because they are married to a pastor (Valeriano, 1981). Many clergy wives see self-disclosure as a danger, something that might jeopardize their husband's career. (p. 563)

Over the years, to reduce the anxiety of pastors' wives and to become more effective in practicing pastoral care in their churches, women with pastoral needs were required to spend time with the pastor's spouse because the pastor wisely decided not to spend time with another woman for fear of leaving the door open to gossip and slander.

Through the intercessions and prayer sessions with the pastor's spouse, a positive relationship would develop naturally. As a result, the spouse's anxiety level would be reduced and the pastor's ministry would be greatly influenced and expanded. For the first time, my life's work of motivating, mentoring, and facilitating seminars and workshops in the leadership arena for the spouses of pastors has been identified through the interpathic personal pastoral care training.

These truths bring pastoral care leaders to the following question: Will I become proactive in the pastoral care of my local church by making an investment in lay leaders and clergy to undergo interpathic pastoral training?

Clinton and Ohlschlager (2002) stated,

> From the client's perspective, it's not worth the trouble to change unless someone-the counselor-is modeling the fruits of a healthy life. Our faith, emotional health, social relations, and marriage and family life must all demonstrate integrity and growth-not perfection or perfectionistic striving, but a humble awareness that we are on the right highway toward the fullness of God's kingdom. (p. xv)

The 25 participants desired to become transformed into the image of Christ. The questions surrounding methods of reducing anxiousness in practicing pastoral care and acknowledging a hunger inside of themselves for more understanding in practicing pastoral care assisted in making a commitment to attend eight training sessions much easier. This project used the Branches, Inc., facilitators to build a bridge for the participants to become transformed. Clearly defined pastoral care training methods helped to reduce a sea of anxiety and to provide a way for individuals to arrive at a safe haven. February, 1992 while working in the admissions office at Oral Roberts University, President Oral Roberts sent a letter of encouragement to honor my partnership with the ministry. On several occasions, I travelled with the Robert's family as a recruiter for the school and observed a light of hope radiating from their conversations with the students (Appendix P).

The words of exhortation through the mouth piece of President Oral Roberts was a light to me and many students that reduced anxiety by listening to his prophetic words of inspiration. A similar light was demonstrated from the Branches Inc., team to the 25 participants of the research project. Scriptures declares, "For God, who commanded the light to shine out of darkness, hath shined in our hearts, to give the light of the knowledge of the glory of God in the face of Jesus Christ." (2 Cor 4:6). The light from the God through the face of Jesus Christ is still shining wisdom and knowledge to students through the professors, administrators, and staff at the Oral Roberts University. Because of the impact of this research project upon my life, the Branches Inc. ministry team will continue shining the light of Christ to all laity and clergy globally.

APPENDIX A

FLYER FOR COMPLIMENTARY COURSE

The flyer distributed to prospects that generated the 25 participants.

Break Free!

A complimentary bible based course
Designed to help you overcome anxiety in person's practicing Pastoral Care through Interpathic Training. Break Free of anxiety to reach out to others and meet your full potentia

8 sessions • 9 AM – Noon
Hope Church Pearland
4209 Broadway Street 77584
6/27, 7/11, 7/18 and 7/25

*must attend all sessions to complete course

Sign up today. Space is limited!

Name: _____

Email: _____

© Can Stock Photo - csp10663613

Questions?	Dorothy Smith-Hubbard	859 907 6457
	drdorothysh@gmail.com	

Appendix B

DEMOGRAPHIC SURVEY ASSESSMENT

TABLE B1

Demographic Survey Assessment

A.1. AGE
- ___ a. 18-24
- ___ b. 25-44
- ___ c. 45-64
- ___ d. 65-74
- ___ e. 75 & Up

A.2. Church Membership
- ___ a. one year and under
- ___ b. two – five years
- ___ c. five-10 years
- ___ d. 10-years and up

A.3. Denominational Background
- ___ a. Baptist
- ___ b. Catholic
- ___ c. Church of God
- ___ d. Lutheran
- ___ e. United Methodist
- ___ f. Pentecostal
- ___ g. Presbyterian
- ___ h. other

A.4. Highest level of Education

A.5. Marital Status
- ___ a. Single
- ___ b. Married
- ___ c. Widowed

A.6. Employment History of Family
- ___ a. Corporate
- ___ b. industrial
- ___ c. Farming
- ___ d. Political
- ___ e. Pastors/Missionaries
- ___ f. Other

APPENDIX C

APPLICATION FOR RESEARCH PROJECT

Application & Consent Form

For Research Project Reducing Anxiety through Personal Interpathic Pastoral Care Training

Dorothy Smith-Hubbard Oral Roberts University

Submitted to Theological Faculty Dr. Edward Decker Supervisor Dr. D. Buker, Reader Dr. Kenneth Mayton

> **RESTRICTED ACCESS!**
>
> **This document contains confidential data that may be reviewed only by Branches Inc. Ministry Team.**

The purpose of this application is to help laypersons develop interpathic skills that will reduce anxiety and the reluctance to practice personal pastoral care in their local church and communities. Each participant will be given the following: Training materials, components and duration of the training courses required. A verbal introduction will provide how this process will work (project, thesis and dissertation).

APPENDIX B DEMOGRAPHIC SURVEY ASSESSMENT

____ a. High School
____ b. Technical School
____ c. College
____ d. Graduate School
____ e. Doctoral

PERSONAL PROFILE INFORMATION

STUDENT #_____

DATE_____

Name_____

Address_____

City/State/Zip_____

Married_____ Single_____ Divorced_____ Widowed_____

Would you consider yourself to be an optimist or a pessimist (i.e., do you tend to see the best in a situation and life in general, or the worst?)?
_____OPTIMIST _____PESSIMIST

Have you ever felt like you were "losing it" Do you presently fear that possibility?
_____YES _____NO

_____

Do you listen to music a lot? _____YES _____NO

What type do you enjoy most? _____Gospel _____Classical _____Easy listening/Jazz _____Country _____R&B _____Other_____

EMOTIONAL HISTORY:

Which of the following emotions have you had trouble controlling or are you presently having difficulty controlling?

(Please check all that apply)

_____frustration		_____fear of death
_____anger		_____fear of losing your mind
_____anxiety		_____fear of committing suicide
_____loneliness		_____fear of hurting loved ones

_____worthlessness	_____fear of_____
_____depression	_____fear of_____
_____hatred	_____fear of_____
_____bitterness	_____fear of_____

Concerning your emotions, whether positive or negative, which of the following best describes you? (Please check)
_____readily express my emotions
_____express some of my emotions, but not all
_____readily acknowledge their presence, but am reserved in expressing them
_____tendency to suppress my emotions
_____find it safest not to express how I feel
_____tendency to disregard how I feel since I cannot trust my feelings
_____consciously or subconsciously deny them; it's too painful to deal with them

Do you presently know someone with whom you could be emotionally honest – (i.e., you could tell this person exactly how you feel about yourself, life, and other people)? ___YES ___NO

Do you feel you are emotionally honest before God? _____YES _____NO

HEALTH HISTORY:

Do you have any chronic health ailments? _____YES _____NO
_____

Are you currently taking any medication? _____YES _____NO

If yes, will the medication interfere with this research project? ___YES ___NO

EDUCATIONAL HISTORY:

Highest grade completed: _____ Do you have difficulty reading? _____YES _____NO
Do you have a high school diploma? _____YES _____NO
In what year, did you graduate? _____
Have you attended a technical or vocational school? _____YES _____NO
Have you attended college? _____YES _____NO
Have you attended graduate school? _____YES _____NO

CHURCH INVOLVEMENT HISTORY:

Please list the name of your church and address where you have served?
Church Name: _____
City: _____ State: _____ Zip_____

List any spiritual gifts, callings, training, education, or other factors that have prepared you for children's, youth, adult, or any other ministry.
_____

List all types of previous community work you have engaged in (Scouts, little league, school activities, etc.) involving children or youth, listing the names of those whom we may contact for confirmation.
_____

Terms of agreement for the research project. There will not be any discomforts or inconveniences in the process of the research. There are no risks involved or medical treatments involved. The participants will not be compensated. Contact the facilitators for additional questions relating to this research. Dorothy Smith-Hubbard is the Supervising Team Leader (drdorothysh@gmail.com). Participants are free to withdraw at any time from the project. There are no conditions that will terminate any participant and each participant is entitled to a written copy of this application and consent form. Adults 21 years and older are suitable for this research. Your signature indicates that you agree with these terms and agreements freely.

_____
Signature of participant   Date

_____
Signature of facilitator/investigator   Date

APPENDIX D

TRAINING, PROVIDERS, TARGET GROUP, COMPONENTS

Training Course	Providers	Target groups	Components	Duration
Pre-Competence Assessment Survey	Branches Ministry Team	Church Membership	Group Presentation	Eight (Forty-five min.) Training Sessions
Christian Formation (Part I &II) Six Stages of Faith (Hitting the Wall) Abiding in the Vine (Ministry of Presence) Applying the Narrative (Telling your Story) Sympathy & Empathy (The Difference) Trio-logical Process (Learning Listening) Process of Interpathic Training	• Clergy • Church Leaders	• Parish & congregational volunteers	• Identifying Spiritual Journey Stages in life of faith Communion with Higher Power Reflecting on pass, present stories and discovering a learning curve by sharing stories	8:30AM - Noon Four Saturday (s) Covering Two Courses per Saturday
Post-Competence Assessment Surveys	• Participants	• Participants	• Seminars • Peer groups	• 1-hour length
Results	Participants	• Participants	• Working sessions	Church Volunteer Opportunities Presented
Celebration	• Pastor	Pastor/Leaders	8 Session Seminars	Certificate of Completion

Training, Providers, Target Group, Components

APPENDIX E

DESIRED GOALS, BEHAVIOR QUESTIONS

DESIRED GOALS, BEHAVIOR QUESTION

(1) Pre (Before) Training (2) Post-Test (After) Training

A. Objectives:

1. I desire to introduce myself without having anxiety.
2. I am learning to shake hands with eye contact.
3. I want to ask questions with confidence
4. I want to have the freedom to dialogue with others in peace.

B. Behavior Questions:

When facing, the following circumstances do you experience anxiety? Please answer the following questions with a Yes or No response.

1. Do I hesitate when I need to introduce myself to others? _____
2. Do I give eye contact when speaking to others? _____
3. Do I greet strangers? _____
4. Is it easy to welcome others into a conversation? _____
5. Do I resist speaking to a group of people? _____
6. Is it easier to speak one on one than to a group? _____
7. Are I afraid to express how you feel? _____
8. Do I perspire when asked to attempt something new? _____
9. Do I avoid meeting new people? _____
10. Do I believe in drawing strength from a higher power? _____

APPENDIX F

INTERPATHIC PASTORAL TRAINING SYLLABUS LESSON PLAN CHRISTIAN FORMATION I

Interpathic Pastoral Training
Syllabus

Christian Formation I

INSTRUCTOR(S): Dorothy Smith-Hubbard Email: drdorothysh@gmail.com
Cynthia Hayes chayescyn@aol.com

I. COURSE DESCRIPTION

Acquaint leaders with the "Personal Spiritual Development Analysis" (PSDA) model for individual personal development. Special attention is given to creating an environment for interpersonal examination that will reduce anxiety associated with practicing pastoral care.

Reference Materials: Dr. J. Robert Clinton, "The Making of a Leader."
Dr. Rick Gray, Personal Spiritual Development Analysis Sample

II. COURSE GOALS

The purpose of this course is to enable the student to do the following:

A. Develop individual PSDA

B. Think critically about her/his own development and spiritual formation.
C. Discover an approach to his/her PSDA that is inherently redemptive.

III. STUDENT LEARNING OUTCOMES FOR THIS COURSE

Upon successfully completion of the course, the student will be able to do the following:
A. Self-actualization and celebration of one's own journey of faith
B. Students will become aware of the transforming redeeming Grace and be willing to offer the same to others.
C. Students will be able to reduce anxiety and practice effective pastoral care.

Christian Formation Lesson Plan Outline

A. Introduction – Christian Formation Part II
B. Sample of Personal Spiritual Development Analysis (PSDA)
C. Major Components
   a. Title page
   b. Generalized Timeline
   c. Running Capsule
   d. Process Items
   e. Concluding Statement
D. How to Construct Generalized Timeline
E. Running Capsule
   a. Childhood, Adolescence, and Adult Experiences
   b. Development and Preparation for Ministry
   c. Ministry and Influence
   d. Concluding Statements and Projects for Future
F. Discussions and Comments Christian Formation, Part II.

I. Each Participant will share his/her Christian Formation (5-10 each) **II.** Instructor will Follow-Up with Encouraging Comments.

APPENDIX G

INTERPATHIC PASTORAL TRAINING SYLLABUS ABIDING IN THE VINE LESSON PLAN I

Interpathic Pastoral Training
Syllabus

Abiding in the Vine Ministry of Presence

INSTRUCTOR(S): Dorothy Smith-Hubbard Email: drdorothysh@gmail.com
Roland Hubbard   rhubbard47@gmail.com

I. COURSE DESCRIPTION

Students will learn the importance of "Abiding in the Vine (Christ), experiencing the ministry of presence and understand the importance of being a loving and forgiving servant in pastoral care.

Reference Materials: The Full Life Study Bible, KJV
Donald C. Stamps, Editor, Grand Rapids, MI (1992)

Text: John 15:1-18

II. COURSE GOALS

The purpose of this course is to enable the student to do the following:

A. Learning and understanding the definitions, symptoms and identifying the root causes of anxiety.
B. Examining the importance of abiding in the vine when administering pastoral care.
C. Learning the theological inferences of the ministry of presence.

III. STUDENT LEARNING OUTCOMES FOR THIS COURSE

Upon successfully completion of the course, the student will be able to do the following:

A. Students will become effective in administering pastoral care and implementing the ministry of presence.
B. Students will effective provide comfort and peace to those in crisis.
C. Students will be able to reduce anxiety and practice effective pastoral care.

Abiding in the Vine & Ministry of Presence
Lesson Plan Outline II.

A. Biblical Account
   a. John 15:1-18
B. Christ Prayer for Believers
   a. John 17
C. Symptoms of Anxiety
D. Statistics
E. Definition of Anxiety
F. John's Example of Abiding in the Vine
G. Incarnation and The Ministry of Presence
H. Closing Comments and Expressions

APPENDIX H

INTERPATHIC PASTORAL TRAINING SYLLABUS LESSON PLAN I. CRITICAL STAGES OF FAITH

Interpathic Pastoral Training Syllabus

Critical Stages in Faith

INSTRUCTOR(S): Dorothy Smith-Hubbard Email: drdorothysh@gmail.com
Karen & Michael Curry   m.h.curry@gmail.com

I. COURSE DESCRIPTION

Students will examine and understand the Six Critical Stages in Faith and learn how to recognize the stages to overcome anxiety in one's life journey to find meaning and purpose.

Textbook: Hagberg, Janet O, Guelich, Robert A., (2005) The Critical Journey, Sheffield Publishing Company, Salem, Wisconsin. Prerequisites: None.

II. COURSE GOALS

The purpose of this course is to enable the student to do the following:
  A. Identify the Six Stages of Faith as it pertains to one's faith.
  B. Process individually each stage as it relates to their journey of faith.

C. Affirm and embrace the importance of discovering self-awareness

III. STUDENT LEARNING OUTCOMES FOR THIS COURSE

Upon successfully completion of the course, the student will be able to do the following:
A. Ability to identify the stages of faith.
B. Experience healing by sharing and through self-actualization process.
C. Reduce anxiety in practicing pastoral care.

The Six Critical Stages of Faith
Lesson Plan Outline II.

1. Recognition of God
2. Life of Discipleship
3. Productive Life
4. Journey Inward
5. Journey Outward
6. Life of Love

A. STAGE CONCEPTS

Fluid and Cumulative Stages
Home Stage and Revisiting
Cages: Getting Stuck or Hitting the Wall
Understanding Stages
Crisis: A time for moving
Similarities and Movements

B. CLOSING TESTIMONY OF FAITH

My personal journey of faith when I had a stroke and hit a wall and how I could move forward.

APPENDIX I

INTERPATHIC PASTORAL TRAINING SYLLABUS LESSON PLAN I. SYMPATHY, EMPATHY AND COMPASSION

Interpathic Pastoral Training Syllabus

Sympathy, Empathy and Compassion

INSTRUCTOR(S): Dorothy Smith-Hubbard Email: drdorothysh@gmail.com
　　　　　　　 Glen Reeves　　　　　　　　　　glreaves@gmail.com

I. GENERAL INFORMATION:

Acquaint students with training designed to help church leadership develop an understanding of sympathy, empathy, and compassion for those in crisis. Clergy and laity's anxiety will be reduced once he or she understands the difference between operating in sympathy, empathy, and offering compassion to others.

II. DESCRIPTION:

The training will motivate believers to reduce their anxiety and address any interpersonal roadblocks to practicing pastoral care with others. The training will also facilitate a positive attitude in leaders toward witnessing the love of Christ in various settings and in specific ways as it relates to sympathy, empathy, and always administering compassion.

III. EXPECTATIONS AND GOALS:

a. Will strengthen clergy and laity to extend themselves in the church and community.
b. It will pinpoint areas of reducing anxiety in Leaders and Laity.
c. Develop a level of compassion that will operate through sympathy, empathy and interpathic.

IV. COURSE REFERENCE MATERIALS:

Stamps, Donald. (1971). Full Study Bible. Life Publishers Intl. Grand Rapids, MI.
Stone, Bryan. (1996). Compassionate Ministry. Theological Foundations. Orbis Books. Mary Knoll, NY.

Sympathy, Empathy and Compassion
Lesson Plan Outline II.

A. Definition (s)
B. Sympathy
C. Empathy
D. Compassion
E. Differences
F. Sympathy Vs Empathy
G. Implementing Pastoral Care with Compassion
H. Old and New Biblical Examples
I. Importance of Applying Empathy
J. Comments and Expressions

APPENDIX J

INTERPATHIC PASTORAL TRAINING SYLLABUS LESSON PLAN I. APPLYING A NARRATIVE STORY

Interpathic Pastoral Training Syllabus

Applying a Narrative Story

INSTRUCTOR(S): Dorothy Smith-Hubbard Email: drdorothysh@gmail.com
Chris Jackson   FWU1949@yahoo.com

I. GENERAL INFORMATION:

Students will gain an assurance and reduce anxiety associated with practicing pastoral care through Leaders facilitating Interpathic training. Biblical based examples and methods will be reviewed, to acquaint students with Interpathic Pastoral Training designed to help church leadership by using a narrative and/or story: The narrative of the Emmaus Luke 24:13-27.

II. EXPECTATIONS AND GOALS:

    A. This training will motivate believers to overcome their anxiety and address any interpersonal roadblocks preventing him/her from sharing their own personal narrative and/or story when bringing comfort to others in practicing pastoral care.

B. Leaders will be taught with an understanding to help others how to ask meaningful questions, situations and context when ministering to the wounded person during a time of crisis.

C. It will pinpoint specific experiences that the leader has overcome regarding sharing their narrative based upon.

III. COURSE REFERENCE MATERIALS:

1. Bevere, John. (2004). Drawing near a Life of Intimacy with God. (pp.20). Thomas Nelson and Harper Collins Publishers, Nashville, TN.
2. Bonhoeffer, Dietrich. (1985) Spiritual Care. (pp. 8-9). Fortress Press, MN.
3. Cameron, Mark (2006) James on the Road to Emmaus, Sylvie Chabert d'Hyeres Publishers. Retrieved from http://.www.codexbezae.perso.sfr.fr.

Narrative Story
Lesson Plan II.

A. Definition:

narrative or story is any report of connected events, actual or imaginary, presented in a sequence of written or spoken words, or still or moving images.

B. Introduction to the Art of Presenting a Narrative Story.

Elements of a Narrative
Setting
Characters
Plot

C. Tips for Effective Narrative and descriptive story- telling.

D. How to tell Vivid Descriptions

   Smell
   Taste
   See
   Hear
   Feel

E. Biblical Books written in Narrative Forms

F. How do you share your story or Narrative?

G. The Importance of sharing your Narrative to aid in reducing Anxiety with someone in need.

APPENDIX K

INTERPATHIC PASTORAL TRAINING SYLLABUS LESSON PLAN I. TRIO-LOGICAL PROCESS AND PRAYER

Interpathic Pastoral Training Syllabus

Trio-logical Process and Prayer

INSTRUCTOR(S): Dorothy Smith-Hubbard Email: drdorothysh@gmail.com
Shirley Jackson FWU1949@yahoo.com

I. GENERAL INFORMATION:

To acquaint students with the Trio-logical Process in that is embedded in the Interpathic Pastoral Training designed to help church leadership. The Trio-logical (Trinitarian Approach with –God the Father, Son-Christ and Holy Spirit operating as the One) approach to pastoral care emphasis on the importance of the unity of the Trinity impact on pastoral care. Biblical based text will be used to support a theme of the ministry of redemption and hope.

Prerequisites: None

II. EXPECTATIONS AND GOALS:

A. This training will motivate believers to reduce anxiety in practicing pastoral care through the Trio-logical and Prayer Process by defining both and how they interrelate.
B. Address any roadblocks preventing him/her from becoming effective in comforting administering comfort to others in time of crisis.

III. COURSE MATERIALS REFERENCED:

1. Bevere, John. (2004). Drawing near a Life of Intimacy with God. (p.20). Thomas Nelson and Harper Collins Publishers, Nashville, TN.
2. Bonhoeffer, Dietrich. (1985) Spiritual Care. (pp. 8-9). Fortress Press, MN.

Trio-logical Process
Lesson Plan Outline II.

A. Trio-logical (Father, Christ, Holy Spirit) (Ge. 1, 2, 3-5, 6-9, 10-11. Psalm 147-148)
B. Purpose and Operation (Creation, Incarnation, Empowerment)
C. Biblical Characters of Two Sisters (Martha, Mary)
   a. Luke 10: 38-42,
   b. John 11:1-44,
   c. John 12:1-8)
D. Works vs Prayer
E. Discussions
F. Closing Expressions and Comments

APPENDIX L

INTERPATHIC PASTORAL TRAINING SYLLABUS LESSON PLAN TRAINING PLAN OUTLINE

Interpathic Pastoral Training Syllabus

Interpathic Pastoral Care

I. COURSE DESCRIPTION

The students will learn the definition and meaning of "Interpathic Pastoral Care. Biblical Case Studies will be presented with a focus on examples of Interpathic pastoral care from a theological perspective. Various Pastoral Care styles, methods, cultural differences will be discussed and reviewed.

Prerequisites: None. Text: The American Standard Revised Bible

II. COURSE GOALS

The purpose of this course is to enable the student to do the following:

A. Identify and understand Interpathic Pastoral Care.
B. Integrate sympathy, empathy with application of Interpathic pastoral care.
C. Review Biblical Case Studies of Pastoral Care Styles and Methods.

III. STUDENT LEARNING OUTCOMES FOR THIS COURSE

Upon successful completion of the course, the student will be able to do the following:
1. Ability to relate to another by incorporating Interpathic compassion.
B. Students will be reassured in their role as pastoral caregivers
C. Student learn to implement pastoral care more effectively
D. Anxiety will be reduced by applying the Interpathic Pastoral Care Training.

Interpathic Pastoral Care
Training Plan Outline II.

1. Introduction:
2. What is Interpathic Pastoral Care?
3. Types of Anxiety
4. Biblical Examples
5. Clinical Examples

I. Definition of Interpathic Pastoral Care

II. Three Case Studies

   A. Father in Law (Exodus 18)
   B. Mother in Law (Ruth 1:15-18, 4:14-15)
   C. Emmaus Walk (Luke 24: 13-35)

III. Methods that Reduce Anxiety

   A. Developing a relationship with God makes a difference
   B. Local Church Membership
   C. Support Groups

Implementing Interpathic Pastoral Care

APPENDIX M

ATTENDANCE SHEET FOR PARTICIPANTS

REDUCING ANXIETY IN THOSE PRACTICING PASTORAL CARE
SIGN IN SHEET

NAME & STUDENT #	JUNE 27, 2015	JULY 11, 2015	JULY 18, 2015	JULY 25, 2015

APPENDIX N

CERTIFICATE OF ACHIEVEMENT

Branches Inc.
Certificate of Achievement

THIS ACKNOWLEDGES THAT

_____

UNDER THE LEADERSHIP OF

BRANCHES INC. COMPLETED

EIGHT SESSIONS OF INTERPATHY
TRAINING SUCCESSFULLY

Pastor Thaddeus R. Eastland,

Hope Church Pearland, Texas, Host Church

_____

DOROTHY SMITH –HUBBARD,
BRANCHES INC., PRESIDENT,

JULY 25, 2015

APPENDIX O

MY DAD'S "EXHORTATION"

My Dad's "Exhortation"
Rev. Winfred C. Smith
July 21, 1926 – June 25, 2014
He loved to recite his A to Z Virtues of Jesus
An Embodiment of Interpathic Pastoral Care

A. He is **ABLE** to keep you.
B. He **BLESSES** us every-day.
C. I know God **CARES** for you.
D. He is your **DIRECTION**.
E. He is an **EVERLASTING** God.
F. He is a true and **FAITHFUL** friend.
G. He is a **GOOD** God.
H. He is **HIGH** and **HOLY**.
I. He is your **INSPIRATION**.
J. He is **JUST** God.
K. He is the **KING** of your life.
L. He is a **LOVING GOD**.
M. He is a **MIND** regulator.
N. We **NEED** him every day and every hour.
O. He is always **ON** time.
P. He is a **PRAYER** hearing God.
Q. He comes in the **QUIETEST** hour.
R. He is the **ROCK** of ages.
S. He is our **STRENGTH** for today and tomorrow.
T. He is a God that we can **TRUST**.
U. He is a God that **UNDERSTANDS**.

V. He is a **VERY** present help in time of trouble.
W. Yes, my brothers and sisters, He is a **WAY**.
X. He has **XRAY** vision. God sees knows all.
Y. **YES**, God loves us.
Z. God has a **ZONE**!

God let's us know that he is our Father and we are his children. AMEN

REFERENCES

Aquino, M. (2002) Our cry for Life. Feminist theology from Latin America. Eugene, Oregon. Orbis Publishers.

Anderson, K. (1994). Baby boomerangs. Retrieved from http//www.leaderu.com/ orgs/probe/docs/boomer.html.

Anderson, R. S. (1990). *Christians who counsel: The vocation of wholistic therapy.* Grand Rapids, MI: Zondervan Publishing House.

Arndt, G. F.W., & Danker, F. (1979). *A Greek-English Lexicon of the New Testament and*

Augsburger, D. W. (1986). *Pastoral counseling across cultures.* Philadelphia, PA: Westminster Press.

Barna Research Group. (Mar. 3, 2008). New statistics on church attendance and avoidance. Retrieved from https://www.barna.org/barna-update/congregations/45new-statistics-on-church-attendance-and-avoidance#.VsaFA5MrI6g Benner, D. (2003). *Strategic pastoral counseling* (p. 15). Grand Rapids, MI: Baker Bevere, J. (2004). *Drawing near a life of intimacy with God* (p. 20). Nashville, TN:

Bonhoeffer, D. (1985). *Spiritual care* (pp. 8-9). Minn, MN: Fortress Press Books.

Burke, P. C. (2011) *Interpreting life.* Eugene, OR: Wipf & Stock.

Carvalho, C., Lopes C., Hollanda I.D., Prado S., Marciano G. C., & Braga, C. (2014). Effectiveness of prayer in reducing anxiety in

cancer patients. Retrieved from: http;//1849l0290364204990.
weekly.com/uploads/1/8/6/8/18686056/spiritual_care_
in_reducing_client%E2%80%99s_anxietyfinal.pdf.

Cava, R. (2006). *Dealing with difficult people*. Toronto, Canada: Firefly Books. Center MA: Andover Newton Theological School Publishers.

Chambers, O. (1992). *My utmost for his highest* (p. 7). Uhrichsville, OH: Discovery House Publishers.

Clark, A. (April 2010). Empathy and sympathy: Therapeutic distinctions in counseling. *Journal of Mental Health Counseling, 32*, 95–101.

Clebsch, William A., & Jaekle, Charles R. (1964). *Pastoral care in historical perspective...* Eaglewood Cliffs, NJ: Prentice Hall Publishing.

Clinton, T., & Ohlschlager, G. (2002). *Competent Christian counseling*. Colorado, CO: Water Brook Press.

Cole Jr., A. (2008). *Be not anxious*. Grand Rapids, MI: William B. Eerdmans Publishing.

Coleman, J. (1972). *Abnormal psychology and modern life* (4th ed.). Glenview, IL: Scott, Foresman.

Coleman, M. A. (2008). *Making a way out of no way*: *A womanist theology* (p. 15). MN: *compassion*. Philadelphia, PA: Fortress Press.

Craighead, E., Miklowitz, D., & Craighead, L. (2013). *Psychopathology, history, diagnosis, and empirical foundations*. Hoboken, NJ: Wilkey & Sons.

Cubreth, J. R., & Brown, L. L. (2010). *State of the art clinical supervision*. New York: Routledge Taylor & Francis Group.

Davidson, J. (2003). *The anxiety book*. New York: Penguin Putnam.

Davidson, J. (2003). *The anxiety book: Developing strength in the face of fear*. New York: Penguin Putnam.

DiClemente, C. (2006). *Addiction and change: how addictions develop and addicted people recover*. New York. NY: Guilford Press.

Didinsky, M. A. (1997). *The effects of instruction on holistic health on self-concept: Anxiety and responses of lay pastoral care ministers*. Unpublished doctoral dissertation, Oral Roberts University, Tulsa, OK. *early Christian literature*. Chicago: University of Chicago. Effectiveness of prayer in reducing anxiety in cancer patients. Retrieved from:

Eleison, E. (2013). Sky McCracken pastoral thoughts.[Blog post]. Retrieved from http://www.revdsky.blogspot.com/2013/02/pastoral-pride-and-leadership.html

Emanuel, L. (2013) UJA Federation Health Annual Conference Report. Retrieved from http://healthcarechaplaincy.org/69-publications/hcc-enewsletter/archives/275issue-84-october-2013.html.

Ellis, A., Joffe-Ellis, D., & American Psychological Association. (2011). *Rational emotive behavior therapy*. Washington, DC: American Psychological Association. Retrieved from https://webcache.googleusercontent.com.

Ellis, A. (2005) The myth of self-esteem. Amherst, New York: Prometheus Books.

Estruth, J. (2000). *Equipping leaders to serve people experiencing stressful situations* Unpublished doctoral dissertation. Oral Roberts University, Tulsa, OK. Fentress-Williams, J. (2012). *Abingdon Old Testament commentaries.* United Methodist Fortress Press.

Fox, P. (1959). *The church's ministry of healing (p.16).* Toronto: Longmans Green and Company.

Friedman, E. H. (1986). *Generation to generation; Family process.* New York: Guilford Press.

Gabbard, G. (2004). *Long-term psychodynamic psychotherapy.* Arlington, VA: American Psychiatric Publishing.

Gerkin, C. (1997). *Introduction to pastoral care (pp.11-27).* Nashville, TN: Abingdon Press.

Gill-Austern, B. (2002). *Feminist & womanist pastoral care theology* (p. 33). Newton Center MA: Andover Newton Theological School Publishers.

Gordon, P. A. (2003). The decision to remain single: Implications for women across cultures. *Journal of Mental Health Counseling, 25*(1), 33.

Grcevich, S. (Aug. 7, 2014). The relationship between anxiety and church attendance. Retrieved from https://drgrcevich.wordpress.com/2014/08/07/the relationship between-anxiety-and-church-attendance.

Greenberg, H. (1989) *Emotional illness in your family.* New York: Macmillan Publishing.

Greiner, L.B., & Bendiksen, R. (1994). Conceptual learning in clinical pastoral education supervisory training: A focus-group research project with recommendations. *Journal of PastoralCare,48*(3),245– 256.

Hagberg, J. O. & Guelich, R. A. (2005). *The critical journey: Stages in the life of faith.* Salem, WI: Sheffield Publishing.

Hakala, P. (2000). *Learning by caring: A follow-up study of participants in a specialized training program in pastoral care and counseling* (Doctoral dissertation). University of Helsinki, India.

Hall, C. A. (2002). *Learning theology with church fathers* (p. 15). Downers Grove, IL.

Hamman, J. J. (2010). "Resistance to Women in Ministry and the Psychodynamics of Sadness." *Pastoral Psychology, 59*(6), 769–781. *healing.* Toronto: Longmans Green & Co.

Helbig-Lang, S., Rusch, S., & Lincoln, T. (2015). Emotion regulation difficulties in social anxiety disorder and their specific contributions to anxious responding. *Journal of Clinical Psychology, 71*(3), 241–249. doi: 10.1002/jclp.22135 Hendrickson Publishers Inc.

Hersh, B. (1996). *A narrative approach to addressing spirituality and exploring personal meaning and purpose* (p. 26). University of Toronto.

Heuristic. (n.d.). In *Merriam-Webster's online dictionary* (11th ed.). Retrieved from http://www.m-w.com/dictionary/heuristic

Hilliard, E. (2005). *Living fully with shyness and social anxiety.* New York.

Hitner, S. (1984). *Preface to pastoral theology.* New York: Abingdon Press.

Hopkins, D., & Thomas, L. (2010). *Walk together children* (p. 22). Eugene, OR. http;//184910290364204990.weebly.com/uploads/1/8/6/8/18686056/spiritual_car Intervarsity Press.

Jensen, R. W. (1999). *Systematic Theology. 2. The works of God* (pp. 42, 90). New John Knox Press.

Johnson, H. M. (1989). *Pastoral care through lay care ministry: A narrative model approach* (Doctoral dissertation). Retrieved from Ruff Library, Atlanta, GA. ProQuest database. UMI No. DP14647

Keller, P. (1970). *A shepherd's look at psalm 23.* Grand Rapids, MI: Zondervan.

Kennedy, M. (2003). "Sexual Abuse of Women by Priests and Ministers to Whom They Go for Pastoral Care and Support." *Feminist Theology: The Journal of the Britain & Ireland School of Feminist Theology, 11*(2), 226.

Kimball, D. (1987). *Power and presence. A theology of relationship*s (p. 7). New York,

Leaf, C. (2007). *Who switched off my brain?* Nashville, TN: Thomas Nelson.

Lee, R. (2010). *Super stress solution.* New York, NY: Random House Publishing.

Lester, C. (2000). *A model of shared servant style pastoral care leadership for lay leaders of the greater Bethany Baptist Church.*

Unpublished doctoral dissertation. Atlanta University Center, Atlanta, GA.

Lim, R. (2006). *Cultural psychiatry.* Arlington, VA: American Psychiatric Publishing.

McFee-Brown. (1986). The essential Reinhold Niebuhr selected essays and addresses. The Composing room of Michigan, Inc. (p.26). Binghamton, NY: Vail-Bullion Press.

McKee, M. (1992). *Deity of Jesus* (p. 11). Kensington, PA: Whitaker House Publishing.

McMinn, M. A. (2005). Care for Pastors: Learning from clergy and their spouses. *Pastoral Psychology, 53*(6), 563.

McNeill, D. P., Morrison, D. A., Miller, H. M., & McLemore, B. (1996). *A reflection of Christian life and compassion* (p. 3-7). Chicago Theological Seminary. Chicago, IL: Christian Century.

Meier, P., Wichern, F. B., & Ratcliff, D. (1982). *Introduction to psychology and counseling.* Grand Rapids, MI: Baker Books.

Miller, R, Baca, J. (2001). Quantum Change. New York, N.Y. The Guilford Press.

Moltmann, J. (1993). *Theology of hope.* Minneapolis, MN: Fortress Press.

Mose, J. (2011). *Pastoral self-care: Maintaining a balance to serve others.* Unpublished doctoral dissertation, Colorado State University, Fort Collins, CO.

Murray, A. (2007). *Abide in Christ* (p. 5). Nashville, TN: Life Way Press. Nelson Publishing.

Nouwen, H. (1977). *The living reminder* (p. 16). New York, NY: The Seabury Press. Nouwen, H. (1982). *Compassion: A reflection on the Christian life* (p. 5). Garden City,

Nowinski, J. (2011). *Hope and survival: The power of psychological resilience.* Retrieved from http;//huffingtonpost.com/healthy-living.

Oden, T. (1994). *Life in the spirit systemic theology.* New York, NY: Harper Collins Publishers

Olsen, David C. (1993). *Integrative family therapy.* Minneapolis, MN: Augsburg Fortress.

Parris, S. G. (2008). *Instituting a missional worship style in a local church developed from an analysis of the culture.* (Unpublished doctoral dissertation). Asbury Theological Seminary, Wilmore, KY.

Pearland Economic Development Corporation. (2013). Education. Retrieved from http.//pearland.com/living-in-pearland/education.aspx.

Perts, C. (1997). *Molecules of emotion.* New York, NY: First Touch Stone.

Rowa, K. C. (2014). *Treatment fears in anxiety disorders*: Development and validation of the treatment ambivalence questionnaire. *Journal of Clinical Psychology, 70*(10), 979–993.

Russell, L. M. (1973). *Church in the round* (p. 17). Louisville, KY: The Westminster and

Salsbery, D. (1991). *Equipping and mobilizing believers to perform a shared ministry of pastoral care.* Unpublished doctoral dissertation, Oral Roberts University, Tulsa, OK.

Scazzero, P. (2006) *Emotionally healthy spirituality.* Grand Rapids, MI: Zondervan Publishers.

Schoenleber, M., Chow, P., & Berenbaum, H. (2014). Self-conscious emotions in worry and generalized anxiety disorder. *British Journal of Clinical Psychology,* 53, 299–314.

Schoff, P. (1994). *Nicene and post-Nicene fathers.* Vol. 7. (p. 102). Peabody, MA:

Seamands, S. (1989). Ministry in the image of God. Division of Christian Education of the National Council of Churches in the U.S.A.

Seligman, L. (1990). *Selecting effective treatments.* San Francisco: Jossey-Bass Publishers.

Sobrino, J. (1993). *The economics of Ecclesia: A poor church is a church rich in compassion.* Philadelphia, PA: Fortress Press.

Stamps, D. (1992). *Full life study Bible.* Grand Rapids, MI: Life Publishers International.

Stone, B. (1996). *Compassionate ministry. Theological foundations* (p. 15). Mary Knoll,

Stone, H. W. (1994). *Brief pastoral counseling: Short-term approach and strategies.* Minneapolis, MN: Augsburg Fortress.

Stossel, S. (2013). *My age of anxiety.* New York: Alfred Knoff Division Publisher.

Tanksley, C. P. (2009). *An applied research project.* Unpublished doctoral dissertation. Oral Roberts University, Tulsa, OK.

Teeson, M., Hall, W., Proudfoot, H., & Degenhardt, L. (2012). *Addictions* (2nd ed.). New York:Psychology Press.

The American Heritage Dictionary (2013). Houghton Mifflin Harcourt Publishing Retrieved from: http://www.yourdictionary.com/psychopathology#websters#d2czjsLQwgXR6JDX.99.

Tillich, P. (1952). *The courage to be.* New Haven, CT: Yale University Press.

Tyson, P., & Tyson, R. (1990). *Psychoanalytic theories of development.* Binghamton, NY: Vail-Ballou Press.

United Methodist Conference. (2015). Revitalization strategy. Retrieved from http.//w.ww.umVitalCongregations.org.

Vine, W. E. (1997). *Vine's complete expository dictionary.* Nashville, TN: Thomas

Webster's New World College Dictionary (2010). Cleveland, OH: Retrieved fromhttp://www.yourdictionary.com/anxiety#X5wtMV5kEDeBTXKD.99

Wehrenberg, M. (2008). *The 10 best-ever anxiety management techniques.* New York: W. W. Norton.

Whitelaw, S., Baldwin, S., Bunton, R., & Flynn, D. (2000). The status of evidence and outcomes in stages of change results. *Oxford Journal Medicine & Health Education Research, 15*(6), 707–718. doi: 10.1093/her/15.6.707.

Williams, K. C. (2003). *Pastoral care for clergy: The impact on new persons entering the A.M.E. ministry in the Southwest Georgia Conference utilizing an attitude and modality of acceptance.* Retrieved from ProQuest database (Order number# DP14690).

Wimberley, E. (1990). *Prayer in pastoral counseling* (p. 94). Louisville, KY: John Knox York, NY: Oxford University Publication

Dr. Dorothy Smith-Hubbard
P O Box 841305
Pearland, TX 77584